The Bounce Back Journey of Parenting

AN INSPIRING COLLECTION OF PERSONAL STORIES

Compiled by
Discover Your Bounce Publishing

DEDICATION

This book is dedicated to all of the parents and carers of children and to the children themselves. May we always find our voices; to communicate, to advocate, to love and to appreciate.

CONTENTS

FOREWORD
By Marvee Woods

Imagine a wild teenager living on the edge of life, thinking that they know it all. Never paid a bill and can't be told what to do. That was me. Playboy, ladies' man, class clown, one of the popular kids. I played football at schoolboy level for Arsenal, Crystal Palace, Fulham, QPR, Leyton Orient and West Ham. I was God's gift and no-one could tell me otherwise. I was on the fast road to nowhere. I dislocated my knee twice by age 16 and discovered my songwriting ability at 15 and decided at 17 that I would quit football and pursue music. I was a reckless party animal wasting my days whilst having fun. No cares in the world until one day I received the call that would change everything.

Two simple words. I'm pregnant. What??!!! How? That was me asking my soon to be daughter's mother, as if I was an innocent virgin who wasn't there playing a part in the moment of conception. Truth is, I was scared. Thinking, 'What on earth will my mum say?' What did this even mean?

I woke up to a call one morning 9 months later. I picked up the phone and all I heard was, "It's happening!" Dumbfounded, I asked my daughter's grandmother, what? "The baby you idiot, she's having the baby! Come to the hospital."

I remember entering the hospital thinking it was going to be a scene from Hollywood, full of incubators and doctors in blue coats and white masks. Instead, I was ushered into a room with my daughter's mum and grandmother and the contractions. No Hollywood. Just us in a silent room waiting for hours for the arrival. I was clueless. Sat there not knowing what to expect. When my daughter was born, I remember at that moment being lightheaded from the whole event. It was surreal.

A year later, my ex-partner, my daughter and myself were living together. My daughter's mother got a job at a popular retail outlet, and for the first time in my life I was left alone with my child while she went to work. I was writing songs at home at this point, so I said, "I'll look after her, you go and work." I'll never forget the front door closing that morning and the silence. I looked at my daughter standing in our hallway with her eyes on me and it hit me…. what do I do now? This was a question that I guess all first-time parents ask themselves.

I eventually figured it out and learnt how to become a parent over time. The routines, the disciplines, the tears, joys, playtime and laughter. Being there for the first words and first walk. Going to nursery and school, sitting in that chair at the end of term getting my child's report, thinking about how scared I used to be on parents' evening. When my mother showed up to my school to see all the teachers who couldn't wait to tell her about my misbehavior during school term (sigh!). Funny how life goes in cycles.

The hardest part of parenting was breaking up with my daughter's mother when she was 7 years old. I was so close to my little girl before this point, and I'll never forget the look on her face when I told her that I was moving out, but I'd still see her 3 days a week and every other weekend. It wasn't the same as living with her and that is one thing that hurts me to this day. The other side of parenting. The separation.

Becoming a dad from a distance was painful for me. It was not the way I had planned happily ever after to be, but not all relationships between parents last. It was better me leaving than having her grow up in a toxic environment.

That experience taught me that kids look at everything you do or don't do, more than what you say or don't say. Action is everything, and if you don't have your crap together, all of your trying to figure out your life passes on to the child via your actions.

I wish now that I had done so many things differently with my first child. I wish that we could be as close now as we were in her early years when I lived with her. I learned so many lessons from that experience.

Fast forward two and a half decades later. I've written songs for Judge Jules, Diana Ross and more. I am now a proud dad of three more kids, so I have four kids in total. Three girls and my youngest son. I would like to think that I've done a good job raising my kids. I now understand that raising myself is the most important thing, because who I am plays a big influential part in who my kids have become and are turning out to be.

I got invited to a business event by my wife. Whilst I was at the event, I got talking to the lovely Nicky Marshall. Nicky and I spoke about everything. Life, business, relationships, generally everything.

Nicky told me about a book she was publishing on parenthood and asked me to speak about my experience as a parent. All the memories came flooding back of becoming a first-time teenage parent. I am honored to be asked to write this foreword. I hope that my experience and all the experiences of every parent in this book, helps someone who wants more insight into the parental experience.

If there is one thing all parents can agree on, it's this. There is no rulebook! No right or wrong way. It's a trial and error, learning on the job situation.

Every child has a personality of their own and must be treated differently. There is no one rule that fits all. Being a parent is a role of helping your child to discover who they are in the world, whilst trying to also discover who you are in the world. It's more than parenting a cute face and changing dirty nappies. It's more than sleepless nights and worrying if you're a good or bad parent in comparison to what you've known or seen growing up.

Parenting is a gift for some and a curse for others, however you want to look at it. Parenting is the beginning of all life and plays a big part in moulding who we all are. It's the greatest job on earth.

Thank you Nicky for asking me to participate in this book. I hope you, the reader of this book, enjoy the chapters ahead. Peace and Love!

***

Marvee Woods was born on May 5th 1979 in Monrovia, Liberia which is situated in West Africa. Marvee moved to the UK with his mother in 1986 when he was seven years old.

At the age of 12, Marvee started playing football for West Ham United. He soon went on to play for several pro clubs at schoolboy level including Arsenal, Crystal Palace, Fulham, Leyton Orient and QPR. Marvee stopped playing football at aged 16 due to a knee injury and went on to pursue a music career.

He now lives with his wife and three kids in Essex and has a fourth child from a previous relationship. Marvee currently works as a songwriter. He has written for many famous artists including Diana Ross.

Get in touch with Marvee:

Website: www.marveewoods.com

Instagram: @marveewoods

"Always kiss your children goodnight, even if they're already asleep."

H. Jackson Brown, Jr.

AMI MORRISON

Ami is in her early-30s, living in Belfast with her husband and daughter. She is currently discovering life as the mother of an inquisitive toddler. In her spare time (if she gets any!) she is a proof-reader and editor for Discover Your Bounce Publishing.

You can reach Ami through the Discover Your Bounce team: info@discoveryourbounce.com

Rationalising the Irrational

Our daughter was born after 37 weeks of a high-risk pregnancy, seven visits to the maternity unit for reduced movement and two in-patient stays. I was first told that she might need to be delivered early at 27 weeks, but she was measuring very small and the doctor wanted to keep her in as long as possible. As time went on it was decided that I would be induced the moment I reached 37 weeks, the point where babies are considered full term, rather than waiting for labour.

I won't bore you with the details, but let's just say it took 4 days and a whole lot of trauma to bring her into the world. She was born weighing just 4lbs and 8oz. I was moved to a ward for women who'd had traumatic deliveries, thankfully in my own room, and spent 3 days there absolutely terrified to be left alone with her.

Our very first night I was trying to express some colostrum around 3am, as we hadn't really 'got' breastfeeding yet. I looked up to see her turning red, completely rigid and struggling to breathe. In a panic I scooped her up and ran into the hallway to look for help. A lovely midwife spotted me and knew exactly what was going on. In the longest minute of my life, she explained that my daughter was so small, the fluid hadn't been fully squeezed out of her lungs during labour and she just needed help getting it out, all while expertly doing just that.

Crisis over, she took pity on me and insisted she would watch my daughter for a few hours while I slept. But how was I ever supposed to sleep again? Who knows what would have happened if I had been asleep? I didn't know it at the time, but the combination of a traumatic delivery and seeing my daughter struggling to breathe laid the foundation for postpartum anxiety.

My daughter had a few of those episodes in the first weeks of her life, but none as scary as the first. Thankfully I always woke up and knew exactly how to help her. Since then she's had the usual falls, bumps and scrapes, but is generally a happy and healthy toddler.

As for me, I was a wreck. A single pin drop could wake me; I was so on edge. If my daughter cried for any reason, day or night, I would rush to meet her every need and soothe her. I would rock her to sleep for hours every day, all while trying to recover from an infected episiotomy and other postpartum complications. Everything had to be done exactly right because there was an awful underlying feeling that even the tiniest mistake would have catastrophic consequences.

I couldn't bear to be apart from her. One time my mother-in-law came over to watch her so I could sleep, but instead I just cried. I didn't want her out of my sight unless my husband was with her, he was the only person I trusted.

Then a global pandemic meant I didn't have to let her out of my sight! No family members allowed to babysit was a dream come true for my overanxious brain. My husband got to work from home, helping with leaked nappies, making bottles and giving me time to go to the bathroom by myself. Sure, the sleep deprivation was slowly killing us, but she was safe. I genuinely thought this was normal. All parents are tired, right? And babies are fragile, so it's only natural to be cautious and worried!

Time went on and inevitably the cracks started to show. I had an absolute dream baby—she never, ever cried. The odd grizzle for a bottle or dirty nappy, sure, but she spent 99 percent of the time smiling, snuggling and just generally being cute. So why was I so angry all the time?

By her first birthday she was crawling and cruising and into **everything**. Completely developmentally appropriate, but the slightest thing would have me yelling. Touching something she shouldn't, knocking something over or even taking too long to fall asleep. I'd go from calm to rage in the blink of an eye. I didn't even know postpartum rage existed until long after I went through it.

I knew I needed to get a handle on this. I just needed a second between cause and rage to make a better choice, but I wasn't even getting a second. My reaction was instantaneous, so what could I do?

In the end I turned to hypnotherapy and it helped massively. It was a light bulb moment for me; I was severely sleep deprived, not from having a baby, but from being hypersensitive to every movement at night. Subconsciously, I was still worried about what might happen if I went into a deep sleep, so my body stayed in a constant state of alert. Once we worked on that I gradually got better sleep and, slowly but surely, my patience returned. I wasn't yelling and didn't have the constant guilt that came with it anymore.

In hindsight, it's so obvious, but at the time I rationalised the irrational. We had a rough start so, of course, I wanted to be near her all the time. She was in preemie clothes for the first four months; she was fragile! It was natural that I was extra cautious. Obviously I'm going to respond to her needs as fast as humanly possible, I want to be a good mother!

My daughter is now two and a half years old and is still a dream, if a little cheeky! I still lose my patience, I even yell sometimes, but that's now my 'check engine' light, and tells me I'm not taking care of myself. I didn't know I had postpartum anxiety and rage until I had recovered, but looking back I can see all the red flags and circumstances that made it possible.

"There is no such thing as a perfect parent. So just be a real one."

Sue Atkins

CHARLOTTE JACKSON

I am a former sales assistant who helped open and manage my local food warehouse store where I stayed for a good 4-5 years. Within this time I also had my firstborn.

Before that, I studied childcare at college which I did go into for a short amount of time. Although I loved my job I had to quit due to the distance I had to travel to and from work. I was thinking of going back to a nursery for work but I found out I was pregnant again with my second. My aim in life is to do a teaching assistant apprenticeship and get into SEN schools.

I currently help out at one of my local baby groups on Thursdays which helps both myself and my youngest to go out and socialise. In my spare time, I love to read and see my family and friends. Writing this chapter has opened my eyes and made me realise how much I value all the people in my life and although times get tough - pushing through to the other side may take it's time but it's all worth it in the end.

Being a Mum to Two Boys and Coping Throughout COVID-19

For as long as I could remember, I always wanted children. At the age of 22 I found out I was expecting my first bundle of joy. It was an amazing pregnancy, I was glowing and I had no problems all the way through. My second pregnancy, however, was a struggle from the start. I was in and out of hospital throughout the full nine months, but the day came when I got induced and my second bundle of joy was born.

Before I had my second, my partner and I sat down and thought it through. I had just quit my job which made us £300 down a week. Could we really afford milk, nappies and wet wipes on top of what we were already buying? We didn't qualify for any benefits and our eldest was still in nappies and just finished drinking formula. In the end we decided it was now or never. We put our eldest in nursery a few evenings a week just before our baby was born to help him understand sharing and also to give him time with other children. We also thought it would be good that I would have some quality one-to-one time with the baby when he was born without feeling like I was ignoring my eldest. Eventually our second son arrived and everything was going well. Until COVID-19.

My partner had a week off work when our youngest was born. We spent the week in and out of hospital and even stayed overnight due to the baby developing jaundice. We managed to have a few days of quality family time, distributing our time equally between our children so our eldest didn't feel left out. When my partner finally went back to work, I started to feel the pressure of looking after two young children under the age of three. He was working long hours and my mum was unable to help me, as unfortunately she caught COVID and was very unwell.

A few weeks later the nation was brought into lockdown. With my eldest now unable to attend nursery and my partner classed as a key worker, I began to feel more and more alone and my mental health continued to decline rapidly.

I remember resenting and regretting having another child. I had thoughts such as, "How can I love him as much as my first?", "All he does is cry", and "Will I ever sleep again?" running through my head. I spent my nights crying and sleeping on the sofa with my baby in my arms just to get some rest. Getting him to sleep in the evening was extremely stressful and tiring. I had to eat my dinner in the bedroom as he would wake every time I left the room. This made carrying out simple tasks feel impossible.

As the weeks went by and my mental health declined, my partner and I would regularly argue over the simplest of things. Issues that could have been easily resolved would often end in a shouting match, adding unnecessary stress to what was already a stressful situation.

I resented the fact that he got to go to work and I had to stay home with our children. Most days I wished he was at home and I was working, just so I could have time away from the house, the area and our children. Something I know he would have happily done but unfortunately it wasn't possible. I felt that our children would have been happier with my partner at home instead of with me as I felt like a failure, I felt that I wasn't bringing up my children with the effort and support they deserved.

Before lockdown, my eldest would often go to his grandparents' house so my partner and I were able to get some rest and alone time. Unfortunately, this was no longer an option and I found myself cranky and snappy; I just wanted to feel like me again. I'd take my frustrations out on my children which I'd instantly feel guilty for as what was happening was out of our control and most definitely not their fault. They deserved so much better from me as a mum. The walls began to close around me as the lockdown felt like it would never end. I felt trapped.

When my eldest was younger, I'd take him to lots of different places. On Mondays we would go to messy play at the library, Tuesdays we'd go to playgroups and Wednesdays we'd often take a trip to the swimming pool. The weekends we'd spend together as a family as my partner was home. I can genuinely say that at that time I was happy, social and making friends, taking each day in my stride. This was not possible with my youngest. Messy play areas were no longer an option as libraries up and down the country were closed. This was the same with all venues of entertainment.

When we finally managed to take my youngest to playgroup, he had turned 18 months. He was interacting with people and children better than I ever imagined. When we finally tried swimming, he was 23 months and it was so much of a struggle. He hated it, often screaming and crying for the majority of the time whilst clinging on to me for dear life. It broke my heart to see him like this. We lasted 15 minutes unlike the usual 30 to 40 minutes I'd spend with my eldest.

After about six months I started to notice that my baby's development was not as strong as my eldest's was at the same age. He was walking but he could not talk. This, I believed, was down to COVID as he hadn't managed to go to groups or socialise with anyone. On the other hand, the incredible bond that grew between my two boys began to lift my spirits. My eldest would often read to my youngest, nurture him with love and attempt to teach him his colours. It was because of this that my youngest learned the colour purple.

I couldn't have been more proud of my eldest for all the help he gave me at such a young age. Things started to look up and I started to relax a little bit more. My mental health slowly but surely started to improve and I started to believe in my abilities as a mother.

Shortly after the lockdown ended, I started to become close to my next door neighbour. She had just moved back in after spending lockdown with her mother. My neighbour was a single parent to a gorgeous little girl around the same age as my eldest, so we would take them out together and offer each other support. We quickly became close and built a beautiful friendship.

On the days where I felt stressed and trapped, my youngest would often sense my stress which would then prevent him going down for his naps, making it feel impossible to complete those very important yet simple tasks. Every effort to get him to sleep would result in tears and frustration. I was heartbroken. My eldest would cuddle into me for his naps, yet my youngest would just cry. "What could I possibly be doing wrong?" I'd ask myself.

My neighbour helped me realise that what I needed was a break, so she would take my youngest and put him down for his nap, giving me the opportunity to spend that much needed one-on-one time with my eldest. At times, she'd take both of them, allowing me to complete those all important tasks such as cleaning my house, taking the bins out, and giving myself a wash.

Because of these small yet consistent breaks, I was able to get everything I needed done and look at the outcome with a more positive and relaxed attitude. This allowed me to offer my neighbour my support and help her in any way I could.

Our children developed an incredible bond and their love for one another blossomed. This was a beautiful thing to see, especially as my youngest had not had the same social opportunities as my eldest and missed out on forming relationships with other children.

My neighbour was no longer the stranger that lived next door, but a woman I considered to be my best friend. To this day I don't know what I'd do without her. She pulled me out of depression and helped me in any way she could even though she had her own child to look after. I gained new friendships along the way as my neighbour invited me to her weekly

Friday girls' night. I was apprehensive at first because I had never been offered something like this before so it took me by surprise. After acknowledging and accepting the insecurities I had, I decided to accept their offer and join them every week. I now class these girls as friends and people I can rely on. Our Friday nights allow me to feel like me again and not just a mother. I can let myself go without having any responsibilities as my partner looks after our children, giving me the freedom I need to work on my mental health. All of this because of a simple "hello" whilst crossing in the hallway. After two years, I still feel like I owe my neighbour a lifetime of debt.

My youngest is now turning two and I wouldn't change anything that happened. The past has made me stronger and I've learnt to appreciate those around me. I love my children and the personalities they portray more than ever. I've also learnt to love others in the process and learn that the world isn't against me. My youngest is still behind on his development as he is still struggling to pronounce his words but he has his ways of telling us what he wants. My eldest is now in reception, he's made lots of friends and his personality is expanding. He has turned into a smart, funny, caring young boy and I am so proud of them both. My youngest is not eligible for two year old funding so I have started teaching him from home, something I have found myself enjoying. He is still slightly behind in his speech but learning more words as the weeks go by. He is learning to count and his personality is blossoming. He is a funny, clever and charming young boy.

I am finally in a good place although I still struggle from time to time with feeling lonely and down, but then I remember everything that has happened in the past few years and how grateful I am that I have people in my life who I can see or that are just a phone call away. I feel stronger than I ever have before and I know my neighbour and my partner have a big part in making this happen. Without them I wouldn't be the person I am today and for that I will be forever grateful.

"There really are places in the heart you don't even know exist until you love a child."

Anne Lamott

CLAIRE CAMPBELL-ADAMS

Having been to the brink of breakdown Claire never wants another mum to feel that alone and desperate.

Claire advocates for mums who identify as neurodiverse/have mental health issues and for those mums who have children with additional needs. She has been on BBC Wales, BBC Radio Wales and in The Telegraph. Claire has also been named one of the top 100 female entrepreneurs in the UK for 2022.

Claire works with mums to help them reconnect and feel empowered.

Connect with Claire:
Instagram: @mumsshoulders
Facebook: www.facebook.com/MumsShoulders
Email: clairecampbelladams@gmail.com

Invisible Mum Finds Her Voice

For as long as I can remember I have had three dreams: to live in America, swim with dolphins and have a family of my own. When I was 16 I went on a student exchange and lived in Wabash, Indiana for a year. Swimming with dolphins would happen when I was 36! But my big dream of having my own family would begin in 2001 when I started seeing Eddie. We got married in 2005 and then in 2006 I discovered I was pregnant with our son, Noah. Our daughter Eden completed our family in 2009.

I should mention, or the kids will kill me, that we also have some fur babies, two Persian cats, Cuddles and Hiccup, and a Chow Chow puppy, Hugsy!

My dream of a blooming pregnancy where I could proudly show my bump and bask in the glow whilst enjoying extra cake was very quickly dashed as I was hospitalised with severe morning sickness on 27th December 2006.

I was about 10 weeks pregnant and scared.

Actually, I was convinced I was going to die. As dramatic as this may sound, I can't stress enough how bad my morning sickness was. I could not stop being sick and retching to the point that I couldn't breathe. I can't really remember the series of events that led me to being admitted to the hospital. I just remember being hooked up to fluids and IV sickness drugs — I could feel the medicine, which felt like fire injected into my veins, travel up my arm as I was sobbing.

We would find out that I was suffering from a condition called Hyperemesis Gravidarum (HG), a severe form of morning sickness. An illness that would be more widely known later when the Duchess of Cambridge would suffer with it. This was 2006 so Kate hadn't even married William yet, let alone raised the profile of this illness, therefore we knew very little about it. It is horrific, not only because it drains you physically, but it also attacks your idea of what pregnancy is. There was no basking in the glow for me, there was basking in sweat after my body had spent hours trying to expel something that wasn't there. There was no eating extra cake or shopping with friends. This was replaced by visits from family with me dry retching so violently that I was gasping for breath. Unfortunately, because of the severity of my reaction, we would need to ask them to leave, all because they had eaten curry and I couldn't be in the room with them.

I was in hospital for three nights during which the care I received was disgusting, had I been able I would have discharged myself. My fluids were being monitored so every time I had to pee it was into a labelled jug, which was left on the window ledge of the bathroom to be tested, along with the jugs from the other women on the ward. There was a blood stained toilet, which was understandable as it was a gynaecology ward, but it was there for all of my stay! Numerous times I asked the nurse to check my IV as it was painful and swollen, numerous times I was dismissed only to find out later that the IV had become dislodged and the fluids weren't getting into my system.

You may be wondering why I'm describing such small details but embedded in these details is the story of my lack of care, both as a woman and a person. By this point it had been decided that the baby was thriving so everything I was experiencing was insignificant.

I didn't know it then but this was to become a recurring central theme running through my experience of motherhood. My motherhood journey, as they say, was to be filled with medical and educational professionals dismissing me as a person and my instincts as a mother. My lack of degree or the fact that I was a stay at home mum would be thrown in my face. Being uneducated what could I possibly know on the subject of my

children's health or education? My honesty about my mental
health struggles would be held against me as me overreacting. I would
quickly learn that my instincts would be swept aside, dismissed as panic and
anxiety, I would be labelled as "one of those mothers" and I would end
up traumatised by the people who were meant to care for and protect me
and my family.

Before Noah was born, my mental health was already suffering. I was
housebound as every time I smelt garlic or mustard I vomited! Being
housebound in 2006 was lonely, there was no FaceTime or Facebook
groups to join where I could reach out to other people going through the
same thing. It was just me and daytime TV. HG was not widely understood
back then, even midwives were woefully uneducated on the condition,
giving me platitudes like, "it's just morning sickness". There was one
midwife that told me, "you are being a drama queen and overreacting!" It
quickly became clear that I was no longer seen as a person by the medical
community, I was an incubator and the baby's needs outweighed my own.
Any questions we had regarding my care were met with "the baby is
okay." Whilst that was a priority for us, once we knew that Noah was okay I
still needed help but none came. When we asked about treatment for me,
time and time again we were told "the baby is doing well"'. This was the
point that we began to realise that I was becoming invisible to the people in
charge of my care.

My pregnancy with Noah continued normally, apart from the HG.

Throughout my pregnancy, my mind was set on not breastfeeding,
however, after lots of badgering by midwives and well-meaning friends,
I met with the local breastfeeding nurse. This appointment was one I will
never forget, in fact it is such a vivid memory I can close my eyes and I am
back in that cubical. Small with two chairs and a table. I was wearing a royal
blue top and jeans, the room smelt like a mixture of tea and alcohol gel and

there were knitted boobs on the table. During the appointment, after she had shown me how the baby would latch onto my breast using a doll and the knitted boobs, the nurse would say something that has never left me.

She told me she would rather I smoke over Noah whilst breastfeeding him than bottle feed him. That I would be causing a life of disease for my baby if I bottle fed! My concerns over my body image and fears of breastfeeding were swatted away as insignificant and selfish. As it turned out, due to the HG, I was too dehydrated to produce colostrum so I couldn't breastfeed Noah anyway, but the voice of this medical expert has stayed with me. I was a failure because I couldn't breastfeed and I was subjecting my baby to a life of disease. Our words can last a lifetime and people, particularly medical professionals, need to be careful with what they say.

Looking back with a semblance of rationale I can see that I was vulnerable and the nurse abused her position to push her own agenda, but at the time it was another thing I was failing at. I had failed at being pregnant and I was already failing at being a mum. I was diagnosed with postnatal depression by my GP. I remember her gently saying to me, "I think you have PND" and I cried, saying, "But I love my baby." I was under the impression that having PND meant I wouldn't love Noah and, oh my God, did I love that boy! I was also terrified that having PND meant that he would be taken away from me. Honestly, this is a fear I still battle with and every now and again it rears its ugly head and I'm sent into a spin.

After years of being off them, this appointment would restart my dance with antidepressants. I had a history of anxiety and phobias but had been off medication for a few years. At this point early intervention through talk therapy would have made a huge difference to my experience of being a mum and my road to recovery. Tablets, while taking away some of the symptoms of PND such as the constant crying and inability to motivate myself, didn't give me a chance to get out all my fears and irrational beliefs. Instead, they were left to fester and like that mouldy cucumber at the back of the fridge that goes soggy and drips, they began to take over. These fears would infect every decision and moment in my life. Giving out antidepressants is not enough, we need to give mums a safe space to talk so fears can be alleviated and forgotten. I didn't realise how much fear and anxiety were ruling my life until I started to talk to a therapist that I would see whilst going through the autism diagnosis process with Noah.

I'm going to skip forward a few years and talk about Coeliac Disease and its impact on our family. Remember that breastfeeding nurse I told you about? The one who said if I fed my kids formula I could poison them? Well, with her words ringing in my ears I stepped into a world where if I fed my kids the wrong thing it could lead to long-term health conditions like osteoporosis and stomach cancer. Cross-contamination became an everyday danger and I would slowly start to unravel.

The diagnosis came with a referral to a waiting list for a Dietitian and a link to Coeliac UK's website. A lot of charities, who have helped so many, are picking up the slack where our NHS is woefully underfunded. What the diagnosis didn't come with was a simple question: "Are you ok, Mrs Campbell-Adams?". I received a few words from a GP, instead of what I truly needed, which was someone to talk to about how it was going to impact my life, about any new fears I had and how best they could support me whilst navigating the news that has yet again turned my life upside down. We were left to wade through the mud trying to work out what on earth we were doing.

Gluten is in everything, even soy sauce! The weekly shop went from us dashing in, quickly grabbing what we needed and leaving, to an expedition that would last hours. Suddenly, we were having to read every label to make sure there was no gluten in the product. Eating out became so stressful that we stopped altogether. A particularly horrible incident in Jamie's Italian in Cardiff would lead us to write to him in The Telegraph. He never responded, we never went back.

A few weeks into our new gluten free life I found out that I had been unknowingly giving the kids gluten. We had been using gluten free bread, which costs a small fortune (400g tiger bread then cost £3.50), but because I had been putting it in the toaster, the bread had come into contact with gluten through cross-contamination. We bought a new toaster that day. As more information came to light we made the decision to make the whole house gluten free. You know me a little by now so you can imagine how devastated I was. The guilt was overwhelming and I couldn't stop apologising. Looking back, this was the beginning of my anxiety around food. I became very controlling and wouldn't let anyone feed the kids unless I had checked it. Something that had been a source of joy had become a source of extreme anxiety. An anxiety that would continue to be fed and grow over the years until I could no longer shop for food and cooking meals would cause panic attacks. If I am honest I still cannot cook without anxiety and I have been thankful that during lockdown I have been able to take a step back and let my husband, Eddie, be in charge of feeding us.

A year and a half ago, I was very close to falling apart. I sat in my therapist's room and sobbed, quoting the powerhouse that is Miranda Bailey (Grey's Anatomy): "I feel like I am being held together with tape and glue." Through everything I have been the kids' advocate. I've become hoarse with the amount of times I have asked for help. I have begged for intervention until my knees wore a hole in the ground. Time and time again I was dismissed, requests for help were denied because my situation wasn't bad or serious enough. One teacher actually congratulated me for having insight which showed I was coping when I went to her asking for help, making myself vulnerable by saying I was struggling with suicidal thoughts!

Over the years I have struggled to keep friendships. I understand why, I was intense and hypervigilant. I needed to always be on high alert with the kids' food and some of Noah's behaviours, which we now know are classic autism traits. As my anxiety and panic attacks grew worse I would often cancel on arrangements or need to leave early. This can grind friendships into husks. Everything we have faced has had such a massive impact on my health, I haven't even talked about Eden's heart surgery! My dance with antidepressants has left me numb and unable to enjoy time with the kids. My hypervigilance and extreme anxiety has interfered with my ability to make memories. A therapist told me that anxiety causes interruptions in the development of neural pathways which create memories. Imagine how many memories we can help women cement in their minds by showing them it's ok to not be ok.

The kids are older now, Noah is 14 and Eden is 12. Sometimes I wonder about the memories I could have had if I had had someone guide me through what was the best and worst time of my life so far. Looking back all I needed was someone to walk alongside me, to encourage and empower me, someone who could see me, Claire, and help me celebrate all my quirks. I now coach mums that feel invisible to be visible and to be present in their lives so that they can create memories instead of living in fear and anxiety. I also advocate for mums who have neurodiversity and/or kids with additional needs, as I have recently found out I have ADHD (a whole other story). We are very often gaslit by educational and medical professionals and this needs to stop. We need to look after mums because if mum is happy the rest of the family will be happy.

Three things I do when I am spiralling into anxiety:

1. BREATHE, sounds simple and silly but try taking a really deep breath, holding it, then blowing out as if you're blowing out candles. Your body immediately starts to calm down when your breathe deeply. Do this a few times.
2. MOVE, get up off the sofa and make a cup of tea. Moving helps me to change my state and concentrate on something else.
3. REACH OUT, call a friend and ask them round for coffee or to go for a walk. Telling a friend that you need support is a sign of strength. My DMs are always open please do not suffer in silence.

Please hear me when I say you are a brilliant mum, your kids are so blessed to have you as their mum and you have so many wonderful memories ahead of you just waiting to be made. Love Claire x

"Your kids require you most of all to love them for who they are, not to spend your whole time trying to correct them."

Bill Ayers

DUNCAN PRICE

For over 15 years Duncan has helped people to achieve their potential, initially focusing on fears and phobias, stress and confidence. In that time he has discovered a passion for helping people turn their anxiety around and learn to succeed 'with' it rather than against it.

He believes that a proactive approach to mental health and self-care should be considered as vital (if not more so) than physical health and is on a personal mission to encourage this change of perspective and eliminate the stigma of mental ill health.

Connect with Duncan:
Website: www.mindaffinity.co.uk
Facebook: www.facebook.com/mindaffinity
Facebook Group: www.facebook.com/groups/empoweryourselfandothers
LinkedIn: www.linkedin.com/in/duncan-price-376425146

Who Learns From Who?

I've often said that we can learn as much from children as they can learn from us. Meeting someone new and going on to start a relationship with her and her two children, in the midst of a global pandemic, has definitely made me realise just how true this is. That said, I didn't expect one of my realisations to be inspired by a ten-year-old stranger in a tree.

I was walking past a group of kids, climbing trees, and I heard one of them say to another that I was her friend's "Stepdad". It made me smile. I've never been one to worry about specific labels but in that moment, although technically incorrect in a legal sense, I felt proud to be given that label. Stepdad—it felt good because it resonated with how connected I feel with the children I now share a life with. How different that life is now compared to just a few years ago. At the start of the relationship I would have avoided that term because of the expectations and 'pressure' I interpreted from it.

If you had asked me when I was younger how I wanted my life to turn out, one of the hardest parts would have been deciding when I wanted kids. I guess I always assumed I would have them. I just didn't know if I wanted to have them young enough so I could still be active with them (and maybe still be active with my grandchildren) as they grow or if I wanted to have them later in life so that I could enjoy my younger years with greater freedom. Well, it turns out there's another option: meet someone new who already has children and enjoy the best of both worlds. I always joke that I managed to walk into the family life, to embrace all the benefits, without needing to deal with the smelly nappies and sleepless nights. In reality I know that I have missed out on some great memories of that time and those key development moments, but I also realise that I am incredibly lucky. I've been able to meet two incredible boys and their mother and make an informed decision to become a part of the family. I've been able to enjoy my freedom, and mature and grow into the person who was really ready to take on that challenge—had I had my own children sooner, then my life would be incredibly different and I wouldn't have been able to make the mistakes that have led to me becoming the person I am today.

My partner doesn't want any more children, so I went into this relationship knowing that its success meant not having my own biological children. It wasn't a decision to be rushed, but as time has gone on it has felt more and more right. I'm truly grateful to have become part of this family.

I've been incredibly lucky to find two great children and a wonderful woman who have accepted me into their life and home. It helps that my partner and her ex did such a great job of raising the children. Their dad is still very much on the scene, as he and my partner share almost 50/50 custody of the children. This means that from day one there's never been any expectation that I'm there to 'replace' anyone or fill the role of father—they already have a great one. This could've absolutely left me feeling like more of an outsider or like I had someone to compete with, but in reality it meant I was free to define my own role as a 'Duncan' rather than slotting into some pre-determined or expected role.

That might make it all sound a little easier than it really was. In reality, I walked into an existing family unit with all the complications that go with it. They had their routines, their ways of doing things and their own traditions. Here I was with no direct experience of parenting, taking on two pre-teens as well as still settling into a new relationship and working on building my own business. I had always enjoyed looking after children. Being an uncle to my niece and nephew and helping friends with young kids is all well and good, but it's not the same as stepping into family life from a place of freedom and in some ways (to be entirely honest) a very selfish lifestyle.

There were lots of questions to be considered in the early stages. The relationship developed quickly. Neither my partner nor I were actively looking for a relationship though we were both in a good place for it to develop. But when is the right time to meet the children? How soon is too soon to move in? How do you know the right approach to any of this? Starting a new relationship can always be a challenge, but when you add children to the mix it tends to add complications. It turns out these things can fall in to place much easier than you might think. My partner was on holiday with the children not far from where I was staying away with my brother so that made the perfect excuse to meet them in a neutral setting, which went well. The timing of changing rules and lockdowns meant things were accelerated and moving in happened sooner than it otherwise would. It would have been easy to get wrapped up in questioning what the 'right' way would be for all of this, but simply taking it all a step at a time worked really well for us and probably saved a lot of potential stress and pressure. I think in these situations the worry about things going wrong can be far worse than the reality. Reminding myself of that definitely helped me navigate my own emotions and experiences throughout.

I went into this situation absolutely expecting that there would be times when the children had to come first and that I would have to be responsible for managing my own expectations and ensuring I made time for my own needs. In any relationship I think it's important to remember that the other person is NOT responsible for your emotions and you are not responsible for theirs. My own happiness is not down to my partner or anyone else— it's up to me. So I was prepared to do what was needed to balance that against the need to adjust and adapt to fit in to this entirely new lifestyle. It was a lifestyle that required planning and organisation, preparation and consistency, quite different to what I was used to. But my partner made it all so much easier. She was brilliant at balancing it all and making sure I felt at home.

I believe that the most important element of the situation, which has made the biggest difference, is our ability to communicate with each other. From the start I have been honest and clear with my partner as she has with me. I've been able to voice my concerns and express my feelings, even when they may be uncomfortable for both her to hear and for me to express. She has been able to share and discuss with me, as we have gone along, and I've had quite open and honest conversations with the boys about how they feel too. Of course, there have been parts of it that have been tough—a child crying because they miss their dad, when they come home to you and their mum, can be really hard not to take personally. But discussing that and being there for him through it has actually made our bond even stronger.

It hasn't all been sunshine and rainbows and sometimes the difficulties hit when you least expect them. I remember the first Father's Day (around nine months after moving in). I hadn't even considered that the date was relevant to me at all—after all, I'm not a father. That morning I realised that I was feeling a little emotional and it wasn't until I reflected on it, that I realised what it was. I didn't expect the boys to think about me on Father's Day—to be honest, without prompting from my partner they wouldn't have even thought about their dad, I don't think. But that day was a realisation that I was choosing to not ever be "Dad". It was uncomfortable and I was sad but it still felt like the right choice—I couldn't imagine not having those special people in my life. On reflection, I think part of the emotional experience was the release of that emotion and the acceptance of that choice. A reminder to embrace what I have and of how grateful I am for it. I'll never be a father, but when I look at what made me want to be one, I realise that I have all of those things anyway. The chance to play a part in helping a young person grow, the connection to other people and the legacy that will live on through them. It's having the chance to learn about myself from them and grow as a person, the reminder to play and have fun—it's all there.

I have learnt a lot about myself during this time and have been provided with a lot of opportunities for growth. I think flexibility has been one of the greatest benefits. I grew up, as many people do, assuming that the way my family and I do things is the 'right way'. Not thinking that other people were wrong, but just not questioning many habits and ways of doing things. That's just how it has always been. Stepping into a ready-made family home, with their own approaches to things, has presented me with countless reminders of this and many opportunities to become more flexible. Simple things that, to begin with, were a little frustrating, for example, how the boys would do certain things, but led me to realise that I was only really getting frustrated because I had learnt to do so based on my dad's reactions to things when I was their age. It's interesting just how many traits of my dad's I began to recognise in myself that I hadn't noticed before. If I'd had children ten years ago, I wouldn't have had the awareness to notice this as much and I definitely wouldn't have realised that I had the choice and the ability to change, in the way that I do now.

I've always admired those parents, especially of younger children, who take a self-first approach to parenting. What I mean by that is those times when a child is behaving in an undesired way and the parent first starts by looking at what is causing the behaviour. Focusing instead on what they can do differently to influence the situation, rather than just on what the child should do differently. That's definitely something I do, but also something I strive to do more and my partner is fantastic at supporting that. The boys definitely offer me more opportunities to reflect on myself and my behaviours than I would have without them and I think coming into a family as an 'outsider' has made that even more pivotal.

In summary, I've been incredibly lucky and my new family have made it much easier than I would have expected it to be. I also realise, with thanks to my partner for pointing it out, that my approach to it has played a part in smoothing the transition for us all. The key elements that have made it work well for me are open communication, working in partnership with my partner, and maintaining and growing awareness throughout.

Every situation has its pros and cons but in reality it's what we make of the situation that matters. Traditional families present as many challenges as the less traditional ones, they are just different challenges. It's entirely possible to build something magical and special that isn't the traditional standard. When you step outside of conventional expectations you are free to create your own reality and shape it to suit you rather than society. I look forward to experiencing how it continues to grow and develop.

"We never know the love of the parent till we become parents ourselves."

Henry Ward Beecher

EMILY JOLLIFFE

Emily is a couples and 1-1 counsellor, specialising in supporting parents through tough times.

She offers tailored wellbeing/autism coaching and small group programmes on themes like setting boundaries with love and working with children's motivations. Emily offers counselling and tailored Zoom sessions to clients in the UK and internationally. She loves walk and talk sessions with those in the Bath/Frome area.

Emily is a certified counsellor in the Option Process Dialogue and an accredited coach with the Independent Authority for Professional Coaching and Mentoring.

Before she retrained as a counsellor and coach, Emily worked in education and conflict resolution.

Connect with Emily:

Website: www.getclarity-letgo.co.uk/

Facebook group for parents of autistic children:

www.facebook.com/groups/specialparentingtogether

Book a call:

hello.dubsado.com:443/public/schedulerGroup/62066a700e964930cc0bf0

8c

Instagram: @emilycounsellorautismcoach/

LinkedIn: www.linkedin.com/in/emily-jolliffe-331b36a

How Our Autistic Child Shaped Us As Parents

I want to share with you my experience as the mother of three children, specifically around parenting our eldest boy.

He was an articulate and funny child, original and often sociable. While his speech enabled so much, there were many social situations where he struggled, became overwhelmed and occasionally he would lash out at people.

At age 7, he was diagnosed as autistic. Though he had no delays, verbally or in terms of regular milestones, he found it hard or impossible to comply at school and many other social interactions were challenging. We'd initially resisted a diagnosis, thinking it would affect how we loved him. In fact, it was immensely helpful in shining a light on ways to show him our love and be useful to him.

Our son had been to two schools he hated. Staff had found him very hard to manage. He did well with one-on-one support, but couldn't comply with the demands of a mainstream classroom aged 7. I was waiting each day for a phone call home as he frequently hit teachers. My husband and I spent late nights on the sofa discussing how to support him in school.

The situation became untenable. We asked what he wanted and listened to him when he asked to leave school and start learning at home. He was initially angry and frequently hurt us or his siblings. He could be very sweet and loving, but also very shouty and had frequent meltdowns. The transition from leaving the house to go out in the car could take an hour.

A friend suggested the Son Rise Programme®. It sees autism as a social developmental issue, rather than a behavioural issue. It offered hope. My husband, Ross, waited to look at their online videos with me; he sensed it could be life changing, which is exactly what we needed.

The Son Rise Programme® is a kind of play therapy, which we did for 5 years. We started small: 15 minutes a day, one-to-one, and worked up to 6-hour days with a team of volunteers we trained.

Our lad is now a teenager thriving in a supportive mainstream school and has finished his GCSE exams. He has a group of friends he sees weekly and is comfortable interacting with adults, teachers and new people too. He's affectionate, helpful and has a cracking sense of humour and curiosity about the world. He's proud to be autistic and we're hugely proud of him.

I'll tell you what changed.

One of the self-soothing, exclusive 'isms' (or stims) that my son had was sucking the ends of his long red hair. One of the Son Rise® techniques was *joining* our son in his repetitive ism, to show him that we loved him without judgement, and build a bridge to his world. By that point I'd done plenty of judging and it hadn't affected the hair sucking one bit! We started curiously joining him when he was sucking his hair, seeing it as a way of regulating or soothing himself. When Ross joined our boy by sucking his collar, as his own hair is short, he shot Ross a look of, 'ah, you see me!' His eye contact was magical.

At our first weekend doing Son Rise® training in London, we committed to 15 minutes per day playing one-on-one with our lad, doing only what he was motivated by and putting aside any agenda of our own. We joined in with him like crazy, read to him, played games and listened to him talk about his passions, namely fishing. We provided low energy to behaviours we didn't want to encourage and we celebrated him massively when he gave us eye contact, shared, asked us about ourselves, or showed kindness.

Over the next year we did more Son Rise® training in London and Massachusetts, US. We extended our programme from one to four hours a day and recruited and trained volunteers to help us offer our boy more. We focused on helping him socially; academics could wait. He'd taught himself to read as soon as he'd left school, we knew there were no barriers to our lad learning! We built his programme up to 6-hour days, like a school day. We trained over a dozen volunteers, both from our local community and students of psychology and education from Bath University.

We didn't have a planned outcome, radical I know! We were there for the journey. We watched to see what our son was motivated by and what he wanted for himself. We rearranged our life to make it easier for all our family: fewer transitions for our son, fewer supermarket trips and birthday parties, more predictability. Our purpose was to *give him* control where possible, rather than imposing it *on him*, as we'd seen that didn't end well for anyone involved!

My husband convinced the Local Education Authority to give us some funding towards running our programme. That was quite a coup. We used the funding to pay for Son Rise® training for our volunteers. We also decided to work less and give our son more of our time.

After 5 years, our boy was 12 and, although he'd taught himself a lot from books, he wanted to learn more as he could now see the benefit of learning from others. He was thinking about starting school. The boy who used to want to live on a desert island! We found tutors for him to help catch up in Maths, Science and English. We visited local schools to find out how they supported kids with special educational needs. We chose one he liked and he started with one lesson a day, building up to full time over a term and a half. The school worked closely with us and were flexible and supportive.

He's a teenager now. He sometimes grumbles about school, but he manages it successfully and has a group of friends he sees frequently. He's been in the scouts, gone on camps and run stalls with his siblings and neighbours. He's keen on Warhammer and gaming, flying power kites and making money.

It may sound like a lot of work, it was! It felt totally worth it because we were empowered to do what worked for our boy. This was dramatically different from trying to work within the system when it wasn't working for him. Either way, we would have been putting our energy into helping him. The way we chose felt constructive and bold.

I now use my family's experience to offer counselling and coaching support to other mums and dads. It's my honour to help parents who want a fearless, heart-expanding way to help themselves and their children, some of whom are autistic. When we, the *parents,* develop these qualities: a compassionate attitude, practical techniques like joining, and resilience through hard times, our children grow too. Their anxiety reduces and they start finding the social world easier. This can increase their language, their ability to ask for help, and say no in words rather than their parents having to decipher their actions. The sky's the limit when we focus on hope and showing our love in useful ways.

What I Have Learned

As David Mitchell (father of an autistic child and translator of The Reason I Jump by Naoki Higashida, a 13-year-old Japanese autistic boy) says:

"Autism parenting is neurotypical parenting on steroids, times twenty. It can get pretty intense. I hope however, it's made me a better person … You've got to be more patient … and not care about the weird glances … you'll be getting from people if your kid has a meltdown in public."

To develop that patience, be a more useful version of myself and not care if people gave me funny looks, I had a lot to learn and am still learning! One of the most important learnings was that someone else's actions didn't define who I am. For example, my son's meltdowns didn't mean I was a bad mum. I dialogued every week (the counselling tool I now offer to others), to uncover the beliefs fuelling my actions and emotions. I could decide if I wanted to keep those beliefs, feelings and actions, or replace them. As with my son, I focused on acceptance over judgement, choices over obligations.

I used dialogues to set intentions too. I prioritised being kind. I set an intention of compassion every morning for years and came back to it if things got heated that day. It was more helpful to me to believe my children were doing the best they could in each moment, rather than move straight to exasperation, my previous default.

I learned a lot about reaching out and asking for help.

There's no way I could or would have wanted to do this on my own. It was vital to give our son more than two ambassadors of the social world. We couldn't have offered enough variety and we would have felt isolated ourselves. We reached out and trained volunteers to be part of a team, over 4 years. Friends and family helped in useful ways, like feeding us, flyering for more volunteers and taking our younger children out.

I learned to lower my expectations: of tidiness, my work output and goals for our son's academic or structured learning. I discovered I'm not a natural goal setter; I'm more open to going with the flow. This has been very useful to help me accept my child, deal with what comes up in the moment and be more responsive. However, where I had room for growth was in choosing and sticking to what I wanted for him. A particular difficulty I had was trying to focus on just one thing for him to learn at a time, as well as setting loving and consistent boundaries. Fortunately, my husband's abilities complimented mine in this!

We worked on social goals like flexibility, approaching it as an underdeveloped muscle and giving our son opportunities to build his. Most of all, we focused on modelling being flexible ourselves. This is useful, as a child with extra needs may be the biggest test of our flexibility, resourcefulness and sense of ease in the face of change and drama we face. What awesome things to practise.

We celebrated his gentleness, turn taking, listening, asking personal questions, joining in someone else's game, trying new things and more. We got good at setting loving boundaries together, and hurting has become a much less regular feature in our home.

I learned about looking after myself before self-care became a widely used term.

I realised my energy isn't infinite and I need time to switch off. Slowing down is good for my soul. I remembered what lights me up: singing, reading, walking my dog in the fields, laughing, coffee, going out, deep baths and yoga. My energy top-ups didn't have to be big things, but they needed to be a regular part of my life.

We also prioritised ourselves as a couple. Parenting can be all consuming, and autism even more so. Instead of those late-night sofa deliberations, we prioritised regular date nights, organised babysitters and tried not to talk about our children! We wanted time for us: the couple who'd fallen in love before this experience and wanted to be together afterwards.

We acknowledged that we had a busy life and a child with extra needs, so we might have more to discuss! We made time for that with Sunday night diary time. There's learning in logistics, discussions and even arguments: how to have these conversations kindly, or how to make up afterwards if need be.

What Advice I Would Give to Parents in My Situation?

- Balance the urge to constantly research your child's needs by setting happy limits on research and news consumption. You're allowed to read a novel, stare into space, drink tea without scrolling, or whatever makes *your* heart sing.

- To spend one-to-one time with your child, find your unique balance between consistency (e.g. 20 mins a day after school every day), and not forcing yourself. It can take a while to build a rhythm. It is counterproductive to 'force' ourselves to do something when actually we need to take care of ourselves first. You'll know what works for you and your child, so listen and do what works for both of you.

- Diet, both nutritional and sensory, makes a huge difference to all children, and especially those with extra needs. We used a gluten free, dairy free and low sugar diet as we saw a correlation of tummy pain and intense energy if our son had those foods. Varied sensory input, arts and crafts, a lot of time in nature and limiting screen use, especially in the younger years, have all been beneficial too.

- Seeing behaviour as communication is becoming more commonly suggested for those working with or parenting autistic children. Still, they are disproportionately labelled naughty or disruptive. We learned from Son Rise® to be 'happy detectives', spending time working out what was going on under the surface and giving our son the conditions to thrive. Focusing on love and acceptance were vital for our loving bond with our son, even when we felt severely challenged by those behaviours in the moment.

- Learning new techniques takes time and a supportive community. We can't consistently put them into practice when we're overtired and under-resourced.

- Ask for help and identify the things you want to build into your life. Without this, we risk burning out and this often-lengthy journey will feel no fun at all. People want to help, they feel good about it, it's how we build community. Again, balance this with you being responsible for your wellbeing. If someone cancels on you, you still get to do something relaxing or fun solo.

- A simple way to approach daily self-care is to create lists of what energises you and what drains you. The goal is to do more things each day that energise you! Plan your day to include a generous helping of energising activities, maybe a walk, tea, bath, slow lunch, cuddle with the kids/pets/yourself, read your book, exercise, whatever that looks like for you.

- Lower your expectations! I cannot emphasise this enough. Don't attempt to do all the things. One goal at a time. I am aware some people feel energised by cleaning or decluttering. (I'm more into occasional decluttering than cleaning!) It's ok to relax before the washing up is done as well as afterwards. There's always more tomorrow.

- Let yourself off the hook. The 'hook' of believing you should be doing more. Decide you're doing enough (there's still scope for more tomorrow). That is a sure path to comfort and ease in the midst of challenges you want to learn from.

These are the main things I've found helpful and wish I'd known sooner! A lot of them are widely applicable and continue to serve me well, years after I'm out of the most intense section of this road. I wish you joy and every blessing on your journey, whether you have a neurodivergent child or come into contact with one in your daily life. They have so much to offer and learn from, when we have the eyes to see it.

"It's not only children who grow, parents do too."

Joyce Maynard

EMMA SPILLANE

Everyone deserves the chance to fulfil their potential, whatever that looks like for them, and in spite of any adversity that life may throw their way. Emma is a firm believer that everyone can move from surviving to thriving with the right understanding and support. The impact of trauma is very real, but so is the power that comes from connection, emotional regulation, greater awareness and understanding, from within relationships and from hope.

Emma is a qualified teacher, experienced trainer, therapeutic parent and therapist, with over 16 years of experience working in a variety of teaching, support and management roles in education, and 10 years spent running her own successful businesses.

She uses her extensive knowledge of trauma and attachment to work with:
- Schools (through training and consultancy) to support them to become truly trauma-informed,
- Adoptive and foster families to help them to access the right support for their children in education; and

- Adults seeking counselling with a trauma-informed practitioner to support them with their recovery, to rediscover their sparkle and to experience living in a way that's much more akin to thriving than surviving.

In her spare time Emma plays the piano, enjoys regular vocal coaching and performing, and is a season ticket holder at Bristol City FC. She is also a big Strictly fan, having grown up competing in old time sequence dancing around the country and being partial to a sequin or two!

Connect with Emma:

Website: www.emmaspillane.co.uk

Email: emma@emmaspillane.co.uk

LinkedIn: www.linkedin.com/in/emmaspillane

Twitter: @emmaspillane_ed

Facebook: www.facebook.com/EmmaSpillaneEdu

Instagram: @emmaspillane_edu

Therapeutic Parenting

When planning out this chapter, I found myself writing with the peacock-themed pen my 11 year-old son carefully chose and bought, out of his pocket money, for me for Christmas. His response when I opened my gift was one of pure delight and it was a precious moment we shared. Through no fault of his own, he has struggled with doing things for others at times and he put a lot of thought into this gift for me.

My 10-year-old daughter has recently been excited about her upcoming Year 6 camp. While I'm well aware of the underlying anxiety that drives her many questions about this trip away from home, I am proud that she's able to even entertain it. The fact that she sees it as an opportunity to go, despite her nerves around being away, shows just how far she has come. We take these wins and we run with them!

My husband and I became parents to our son and daughter through adoption. Our children experienced adversity in their early years within their birth family, to such a level they were removed from their care. Suffice to say that in these circumstances children, more often than not, develop attachment issues and are impacted by the trauma they've been through. They develop a different view of the world than those who've had nurturing, secure attachment experiences, or who have received 'good enough' parenting and support in the face of adversity. As a result of their life experiences, our children need us to parent them therapeutically. As adoptive parents, our duty of care is to support them to heal from their trauma within the context of our family relationships, alongside all the usual things that parents do.

When we welcomed our children into our lives, we didn't really get the honeymoon period that some adoptive parents report in the early days. It was full-on; emotional dysregulation, separation anxiety, push-pull, rejection, extreme self-reliance, overfamiliarity with strangers, lots of anger and frustration, and everything laid bare from day one. It was tough for everyone, especially for the children. A completely understandable response to moving across the country to a new place and leaving their foster home to live with yet more new people. People who they had only met a handful of times prior, but had already chosen to call Mummy and Daddy. We were fortunate that my husband was able to take the first 4 months off of work to help us all with bonding as a family, but of course when it was time for him to go back to work, it was a big adjustment for everyone (and triggered loss and change again for our children).

While alone at home with our children, for a long time I couldn't be in a different part of the house, or walk out of the back door to the tumble dryer in the garage without my children screaming the house down. I got used to telling the children where I was going every time it looked like I needed to leave the room and when I'd be back, but the separation anxiety was off the scale. Night times were also tricky as their anxiety peaked at bedtime, and for a long while we were unable to leave the children unsupervised together in a room as they struggled with their dysregulation and took their distress out on one another. I'll be honest, in that first year or so I felt overwhelmed, exhausted and doubted my parenting ability countless times. Reflecting back over the past seven and a half years, it's hard to pinpoint just one or two things which have really helped us all progress, build trust and get to where we are now. We are much more about thriving rather than surviving in our little family unit now, mostly due to a few considerations…

Putting the Children's Feelings of Safety and Emotional Regulation at the Heart of Everything

Routine, consistency and repetition have served us well. Our children cope best when they know what's coming next, and can hook in to anchors throughout the day. Morning, mealtime and bedtime routines have all played their part in creating a safe framework from which to build on. We had to get comfortable with the idea of not being spontaneous very often. This was especially hard in the early days, as we just wanted to give the children lots of fantastic opportunities and fun, but they weren't able to cope. We needed to go right back to basics and keep life as predictable and simple as possible. They would show us how overwhelmed they were through sabotaging their experiences. It took us a while to attune to the smaller anxiety cues that we now recognise instantly, that allow us to intervene earlier and prevent things from escalating.

It wasn't easy to maintain what felt like incredibly mundane routines and minimal change while we all adjusted to being Family Spillane. There is also the point that everyone naturally wants to meet your children which adds even more pressure during a time when it is equally important to stay within your bonding bubble. Doing too much out of the usual routine can still be challenging, but, as part of expanding our childrens' windows of tolerance, we occasionally do something which involves staying out a bit later, or requires our routines to be out of whack for a bit. When it feels right to do so we increase the frequency of these changes or duration of outings. When we prepare to push outside of the children's usual comfort zones we accept that the children will need a lot more preparation than usual, that there will be a strong need for more reassurance and support during and after the experience.

The sense of knowing when enough is enough in the moment and being flexible with leaving places early helped. Our habit of always forewarning friends and family that we might need to make a sharp exit from play dates or parties has made it a whole lot easier to manage.

A safe and steady presence throughout whatever life throws at us is paramount, as is containment, and an expectation that there will be times we just need to ride out the storm. Through this we come out stronger and our children learn that we are truly there for them through thick and thin. Trusting that holding firm, being present and consistent will pay off, has kept us steadfast. Even though when you're riding out one of those waves it can feel all-encompassing it is never more important to find and hold a safe, calm space.

Self-compassion and Not Being Afraid to Seek Support When Needed is a Must

We have learned that it's incredibly important for us to manage our own emotional regulation and tend to our own needs in order to be able to maintain a calm presence as much as possible; in order to co-regulate we must self-regulate. I can still struggle with parent guilt over prioritising my own needs from time to time, but when I don't take time for myself it impacts the whole household.

I've also regularly sought support over the years as and when needed – via counselling, holistic therapies, quantum energy coaching, adoption support groups, and of course through talking things through with friends and family. Parenting children with developmental trauma leaves you at risk of compassion fatigue or blocked care if you don't look after yourself. It's not always been easy to ask for help, however, I have always felt better for having reached out and accepted support.

The joy we experience doesn't get diminished when we parent children with attachment difficulties, but it can be especially exhausting at times. Any change can lead to a wobble, and a wobble can quickly trigger the stress response and survival mode for our children. I know that my level of regulation hugely impacts how my children cope – if I am steady and reassuring, I can support them through co-regulation and they are more able to manage their day to day as a result; when I'm dysregulated it has the opposite effect.

Studying the neuroscience around the impact of trauma on the brain has been especially helpful in terms of knowing what's going on for our children and how we might best support them along the way. It's also been key to understanding that progress may be slow, as we are quite literally aiming to support our children through rewiring their brains, and challenging core beliefs. Knowing that progress is likely to be slow means we celebrate the small wins and are better able to manage our expectations (both of ourselves and our children).

Since becoming a mum through adoption I've also needed to reflect on my own attachment patterns and dominant style, as well as my own triggers. The interplay between our different attachment styles within the family can be very apparent at times, but having awareness around that has been incredibly helpful.

Honesty and Openness About Birth Family and Adoption

We've been open with the children since the first day we became a family that they were adopted, so conversations around their birth family have never been taboo and it's common for comments to creep in to normal conversation. In fact, when my daughter was around 5 years old, she decided she wanted to ask some questions about her birth family, loudly, in the bread aisle at the local supermarket. I was mindful of managing that conversation so as not to shut it down, but equally we didn't really want the stranger in aisle three knowing our daughter's life story! Over the years, the most interesting questions have popped up while we've been driving along in the car – we think this is because: a) car journeys are very regulating so the children generally feel safe and calm when we're out driving around, b) there's less eye contact than in a normal face to face conversation and c) the children are off screens, away from distractions at home, in a more mindful space and able to notice the thoughts whirring around in their heads. We sometimes get questions from the children we can't answer, but now that they are a bit older, we're able to agree on some questions to put in our next letter to their birth family (we have letterbox contact twice every year). This level of openness and honesty has been hugely important in terms of building trust between us and our children, and is an ongoing part of life story work, which is something else we committed to when we were approved to adopt.

Share the Load

We're fortunate to be surrounded by very supportive friends and family who have welcomed our direction and information, which has helped us throughout our family journey. At times, however, it can be isolating to parent children who have experienced early trauma, as the level of understanding in our current society isn't as good as it could (or indeed should) be. There are still many myths circulating around adoption, perpetuated by the media, mostly around the 'happy ever after' narrative and a distinct lack of understanding of the impact of early trauma on the developing child. As a result, I learned quickly that I'd need to become a firm advocate for my children in pretty much every area of life. In our dealings with nursery, school, extra-curricular clubs and other health professionals to name but a few, their understanding of attachment and trauma has been hit and miss. It's been up to me in many cases to explain what's going on for my child, to clearly articulate their support needs, to read between lines based on previous experience and pre-empt situations in an effort to avoid triggers and issues further down the line. It's what's inspired me to go out and deliver training in the education sector; but in relation to my role as a parent. I've done it so often and consistently enough that my children know I have their back and I'll advocate for them, as appropriate, to ensure they get the support they both need and deserve.

It really has helped to keep in touch with other adopters, from right at the beginning when we decided to pursue adoption, through to living life in our adoptive family unit. Having others who understand the lingo and 'get it' instantly when you share some of your challenges around letterbox contact, life story work, therapeutic interventions, attachment issues, or 'Pupil Premium Plus' funding (to name a few) is invaluable. We also don't ever have to face those awkward moments with one another where someone raises a conversation about pregnancy, birth or asks why we chose our children's first names (we didn't – they were chosen by birth family and the children have kept them), as we might when talking with biological parents. We've taken the children to several events with other adopted children over the years, and you can see that more often than not the children also 'get' one another – there's an unspoken understanding in the way they engage with one another. Connecting with others in similar situations has been so important for all of us.

Expressing and Sharing Joy and Gratitude

As our children head into their teen years, we know that this is likely to be an intense few years where identity will naturally take centre stage. Already tricky for children who were raised by their biological families, it can be especially complex for adopted children. Going forward we will continue to notice those special moments, however fleeting, out loud together, to appreciate just how far we've all come and hope that no matter what waves we need to ride out in future, our children know that we've 'got this' together.

"There's no way to be a perfect mother and a million ways to be a good one."

Jill Churchill

HANNAH MURPHY

I am a caring, kind and empathetic individual who has a passion for learning new things. Growing up in Spain and experiencing another way of life, really helped to shape who I am today.

After my grandmother was diagnosed with terminal cancer, I moved in with her to give her emotional support as well as help with household duties. I realised I was passionate about helping others and so I applied for a job working within the care sector. I loved this job and really found helping others extremely rewarding.

I became a mother at the age of 21 and took a break from work to focus on her needs and upbringing.

I now work as a social media marketing assistant from home which allows me to work around my daughter's needs comfortably. Since working this job, I have become a very creative person and enjoy writing blogs on common wellbeing topics.

Connect with Hannah:

Linkedin: www.linkedin.com/in/hannahmariemurphy

Being A Mother And Coping With Anxiety

Growing up, I always admired my mum and the confidence that shone through her. The bond she had with each and every one of her four children was strong and beautiful. I remember always wanting to be like her more than anything, so it probably comes to no surprise that I always envisioned having children and giving them what my mother gave us.

I used to always be a very confident and outgoing child, often being referred to as a 'bull in a china shop' by my mother. I would stand up in front of a crowd and sing my little heart out without a second thought. Over the years, however, that confidence slowly died and the anxiety grew, causing me countless sleepless nights.

In 2003, my parents told me and my two siblings that we would be moving to Spain. My mother was pregnant at the time and relied on my grandmother's support with bringing up three children, all under the age of six.

My mother didn't want to leave my grandmother and so for this reason, we moved to a beautiful village in the Costa Blanca region with our grandparents. The five-bedroom, two-story house was located in the middle of a pine forest. The scenery was beautiful, and the climate would allow us to have hours and hours of family fun. It's safe to say that we had the most amazing childhood. We embraced the traditions and culture and thrived. I thrived.

In 2007, my parents separated, and my father moved out of the family home. My mother was left to manage 70 hour weeks, working three different jobs, all whilst being an amazing and inspirational mother who gave each and every one of us unconditional love.

Why wouldn't I want to be like my mother? She's an incredible, selfless person who has nothing but love to give.

After 4 years of working endlessly and sacrificing her happiness just to keep a roof over our head, it was no longer possible to stay in Spain. In 2011, my mother made the decision to move us back to the UK. This is where my anxiety began.

We moved to a village in Weston-super-Mare to be near my uncle and auntie and my siblings and I started school soon after. My brothers and sister fitted in quite well, and they adapted quickly to our new life. I, on the other hand, struggled to let go of my old friends and fit in with the English children. We had different humour, different taste in music and different hobbies. I felt so out of place and I guess I'd always hoped this new life would only be temporary.

Despite this, I was confident and happy with who I was, until the bullying started.

I still remember their faces, looking at me and laughing. I remember the confusion and embarrassment of not understanding what I had done wrong.

When I finally got home and logged onto Facebook, I found hundreds of negative comments on my latest upload, "Get your bra out" being the main catchphrase. I had uploaded a picture in which the corner of my bra was showing. Did I really deserve this? Whether I did or not, it was relentless, and their words hurt nonetheless.

The bullying continued for what felt like an eternity and I felt so alone. My friends in Spain seemed to have forgotten me and carried on with their life. We were rarely in touch and life in the UK was becoming my reality.

In 2012, our landlord made us homeless and my mother was forced to move us again to emergency accommodation in Bristol. Our grandparents were nearby so we would usually spend the days with them and the evenings in our tiny little flat that consisted of three beds, a kitchen and a toilet. Despite the bullying being over, the fear of judgement from others would continue and affects me until this day.

Soon after, we were put into a new school, where I met some amazing people, including one very special person who was even at the birth of my daughter. Things were getting better and I finally started to find my place again.

In 2015, whilst in a very controlling and toxic relationship, I had a miscarriage. I started to question myself and my ability to make good life choices. I felt like a failure, with every attempt at happiness ending miserably. I hated myself for not being good enough. I must've done something wrong and that's why my baby didn't survive. That's why my relationship didn't work and that's why I kept falling short. All of these thoughts only contributed to my anxiety and how I felt toward myself. Losing my baby however, only made me want to be a mother more than I ever had before.

Some time passed and in 2016 I was in a new relationship. However, it didn't work out and in early 2017, I found out that I was pregnant shortly after we split. I was 8 weeks along and I hadn't really spoken to my ex in a while, as we weren't on speaking terms. We got back together shortly after the first scan. This relationship wasn't right and I knew I had to do what was best for my baby who I already loved so much. We made a final decision to co-parent separately shortly before she was born.

I remember when she was born, holding her for the first time, the pure love and emotion I felt towards her. Blissful in so many ways. She was the answer to my prayers, or so I thought. Despite her being the best thing that had ever happened to me, it hit me quite soon after like a slap in the face that this was not as easy as I had thought it would be.

My anxiety didn't just go away, if anything it got worse because now I had a small, beautiful little girl to think about. Those thoughts about not being good enough would come back stronger than ever. This wasn't helped by my milk production slowing down. I felt even more like a failure and found the transition from breast to formula extremely hard and I worried about our bond.

"What if she stops loving me because I can't give her what she needs?" I'd ask myself.

The health visitor suggested that I attend a baby massage course, as studies had shown that this could help manage stress and anxiety in mothers and babies. We all lived under the same roof and my sister decided to come along to support and help me. She knew how much I struggled, so brought my niece who was born 10 weeks before my daughter. I was under the impression that this group was small and it would help manage my anxiety. However, it had the opposite effect and I hated every second of it. This made me realise, through this and other experiences, that I had huge anxiety around others I didn't know, even more so in groups.

The times we had to sit in a circle and talk to the group or when we would sing… I felt stupid, on edge and judged and wanted the ground to swallow me whole.

My daughter's dad stayed in the picture until she was six months old when he suddenly stopped showing up to see her. He'd missed a few weeks here and there and struggled with his own problems, but he'd never gone more than 4 weeks at a time without at least seeing her. He disappeared from her life altogether.

Soon after, my daughter and I moved into our very first home. Her dad wasn't around and I no longer lived with my mother. The weight of managing my anxiety and bringing up my daughter on my own began to close in on me. My family and friends really helped me as much as they could, but those internal thoughts of "What if I'm not good enough for her?" started again and were louder than ever.

I settled well despite the anxiety and things were starting to look up.

I got into a long-distance relationship with a family friend who lived in Spain. He was lovely and really showed me what a healthy relationship looked like. Me and my daughter would often go out to Spain and stay for a couple of weeks at a time with him and his very welcoming family. I remember stepping off the plane and feeling like I was home, and dreading coming back to my actual home and my reality. I suddenly thought of how much I wanted to give my daughter the same childhood I'd had and became obsessed with the fairy-tale. I was asked to move out there, my partner and his family would have supported me and my daughter and they would have helped me find a job that would work around being a parent. But I couldn't do it, I would have to give up our home that I was lucky to have got and put everything on the line, and I couldn't risk losing everything. I couldn't risk letting my daughter down.

When the pandemic started, it brought many ups and downs. It became impossible to travel abroad to see my partner, so naturally, the relationship came to an end. I had however moved back in with my mother as the mere thought of not being able to see her for weeks on end scared me to death. We had a lovely lockdown, the weather was beautiful and we spent most of our time in the garden with my mum making her famous Mojitos.

My grandmother had passed away the previous summer and this year really forced us to be together and appreciate what we had. My mother helped me with my daughter and my anxiety, for the first time in forever, quietened. It no longer consumed my every thought because I had my mum, my best friend.

My brother and his partner moved to Spain in August 2020 and we were able to fly abroad again, so we flew out to Spain for a big family holiday to see them. This was the first time in over 10 years that we had all gone back to Spain together. Two and a half weeks of pure fun. My daughter and niece loved every single second of it. It was on this holiday, that I finally let go of my life in Spain and realised that I already had everything I needed.

When lockdown ended, I had to face reality again. Moving back into the flat with my daughter felt so strange and, at first, I struggled to adapt to it just being me and her again. I would've quite happily stayed at my mother's, but I knew that I had to go home. Not long after, my neighbour and I started to talk and we got pretty close quite quickly. She had two young boys, one who was close in age with my daughter and one who was born just before COVID-19 struck. I'd often take care of her youngest and put him down for his naps, so she could have one-on-one time with her eldest. In turn, she would take my daughter so I could have a shower or tidy up the flat. We'd spend the days together and built a strong support bubble for each other and our children. Things became a little easier.

Over the last year, my outlook on life has completely changed. Although I still suffer from anxiety, I have learnt to speak to those closest to me. I have learnt that the thoughts are just thoughts and that I am a strong, independent, loving and caring person. People won't always be kind and people won't always like me. But that's ok, I like me and that's what matters.

I have a job now that really requires me to connect with my creative side and go with my intuition. I am learning new things every day and finally feel supported at work, with my mental health being something my employer prioritises. It is showing me that I am capable of anything and that the world is my oyster. For this, I am truly grateful.

I have built new friendships and strengthened existing ones, spent crucial time with family and I'm still learning how to be a mother with anxiety, with my daughter by my side every step of the way. My daughter is a bubbly, funny and intelligent little girl, she loves playing with my hair and eating anything sweet. I know I am doing the best I can, and I couldn't be more proud of my baby even if I tried. She doesn't always like me, especially at bedtime, but we love each other unconditionally and I wouldn't change that for the world. I still struggle to take her out on my own, but I do it, which is something I never thought I'd be able to do. I took her to the cinema for the first time quite recently to watch Clifford the Big Red Dog and she loved every single second of it, nearly as much as she loved the popcorn. Seeing her so happy is honestly what makes me most happy.

Soon she will be starting school and I know that with school comes many other worries, especially as my experience with it was quite traumatic. But we both have each other, my amazing mother and siblings and so many more incredible and supportive people. So even though I can admit I'm scared, I can also admit that I'm excited. Excited for the next chapters in our life.

"We may not be able to prepare the future for our children, but we can at least prepare our children for the future."

Franklin D. Roosevelt

HELEN HYDE

Helen Hyde is a videographer who lives in Gloucestershire with her husband and young daughter. She started her working life as a BBC Journalist before launching her own media production company, Hyde Media after finishing maternity leave. Helen now specialises in smartphone filming and has recently curated an online course for other small business owners to discover how to make professional looking videos for social media using their own phones. She built Maternal Balance, together with her husband, in their 'spare' time during Lockdown. The site is full of free resources, including pilates classes, breathing and mindfulness techniques, postpartum exercise, and nutrition tips all designed for pregnant women and postnatal mums struggling with anxiety.

Find out more about Hyde Media at www.hyde-media.co.uk or follow @hyde_media on Instagram.

Find out more about Get Social with Video at www.getsocialwithvideo.com And discover Maternal Balance at www.maternalbalance.co.uk

Maternal Balance

For the first year of our daughter's life, I bounced along with the usual ups and downs of new parenting. Everything about the situation was alien to me, but as long as I left the house once a day every day, spoke to someone, did some exercise, and had the solace of our NCT WhatsApp group, I could cope. Of course, there were days when she wouldn't stop crying. There were days when I wouldn't stop crying. Sleep regressions, an emergency c-section to recover from, mastitis…and boredom – no one ever talks about how boring it can be at times when you've come from a busy, active, independent life and working full time. But the downs were met with ups, and we had a lot of fun together.

Of course, I was tired, very tired. Then one day, I was driving to a nearby town around 5 miles away, with my daughter happy babbling in the back. I parked up the car and realised I couldn't have told you a single twist or turn of the journey I had just made. Many of us often drive on autopilot, especially when we're knackered. But this was a whole new level of oblivion. A fog. And I found it quite scary.

I had recently returned to work and my mental capacity had to quite suddenly switch from a year of soft play and adventure playgrounds to emails, meetings, and decisions. I am a freelancer and took on two separate jobs at once, one of which was a new direction for me and was becoming increasingly stressful. I found myself awake in the middle of the night, sending email reminders to my own inbox or even replying to people. I had put pressure on myself to perform to a full-time level in this new role, whilst doing two part-time jobs.

This combination of exhaustion, stress and worry was giving me anxiety. Only I didn't know it at the time. I had always been incredibly lucky with my mental health and had never experienced the sensations I was feeling.

The car journey was a bit of a wake-up call, without realising what was happening. I visited my GP; an incredibly softly spoken woman with children of her own, who looked at me and listened. It is so hard not to cry in front of someone like that. I'm not sure why I didn't. I could have, she wouldn't have minded. But I think I was still in this self-determined ideal of being a professional worker, no longer a full-time mum. I don't break down in front of people.

She recommended exactly what I needed – help! In the form of talking therapy with a wonderful psychotherapist who specialised in maternal mental health. I have never underestimated the power of just talking to someone about what you are experiencing, someone objective, outside of your circle, who will listen. And instead of reliving what I was experiencing, we looked to the future, also known as coping mechanisms.

She helped me to understand how 'normal' it was to feel the way I was feeling. I put the word 'normal' in inverted commas because I am still unsure whether this is the right word to use. I understand that using it helps others to think it's ok to experience what they're feeling. But is it normal to feel maternal anxiety a year after the birth? Should something be termed normal just because a lot of people are feeling it? I worry that it potentially stops people getting the help they need early on.

My anxiety has always manifested itself in an incredibly physical way, which is quite strange to experience, although also very 'normal'. I know it's coming because I feel it in my eyes first. I can't look at my phone screen, it actually hurts my eyes. My heart beats a little bit too fast and I feel like I am only breathing from the very top of my lungs. And then my body actually clenches up. I walk like I'm in my nineties, hunched over, slow, and shiver like it's freezing cold in the house. Afterwards, I feel so, so tired. Like that bout of anxiety has taken everything it can from of me.

One of the most prominent mental effects I feel is something called

Intrusive Thoughts. Intrusive Thoughts aren't spoken about a lot, they're not really mentioned in the realm of motherhood, and it makes the thoughts seem a bit of a taboo. Have you ever driven down the road and thought, "What if I just swerve and send the car over the edge of the cliff?" Or held a newborn baby and thought, "If I just open my arms now it will drop to the ground."

I was so relieved to read about these thought patterns in a book I highly recommend, written by comedian Robin Ince. 'I'm a Joke and So Are You' is described as a comedian's take on what makes up being human. It's an enlightening and engrossing read. His take on Intrusive Thoughts is that it's actually our brain prepping us for danger. It's telling us, if you don't concentrate on the road then you could accidentally swerve off the edge of the cliff. Or if you don't hold your friend's newborn baby tightly, you could easily drop it. I liked this positive slant on what was happening inside my head. It brought relief and understanding to me.

My Intrusive Thoughts were always centred on my daughter, of course. It's to be expected in the first few months. Almost every parent will experience anxious thoughts during the perinatal stage – that time just before or after giving birth. Particularly that awful dread of cot death, walking into a silent bedroom in the morning. It's very natural to worry about your child, you want to keep them safe. But when these thoughts continue after months, or even years, that's when it's not 'normal'. It happens to me when I am more tired than usual, can't sleep for stressing about work, or know that anxiety is on its way. The thoughts are horribly vivid, and always involve ponds or busy roads…and my daughter.

The problem is, as my psychotherapist explained, once you give Intrusive Thoughts time in your mind, they pop up more often. It's a catch 22 situation. You thinking about something signals to your brain that it must be important, and therefore your brain tells you to think about it more! Instead, she taught me to put my thoughts onto a train and watch them 'choo choo' off down the track. You don't have to choose trains, you could choose a car, a boat, a bike, whatever fits with you. I'm a closet steam engine fan, so I choose to watch myself pop the thought into a railway carriage and puff off into oblivion. It works, try it!

I'm not generally one for talking about my health, but as I started to understand and cope with what I was feeling, I started speaking to my other mum friends. What struck me, and struck me hard, was how many of them had also experienced anxiety. It led me to build Maternal Balance during lockdown. At the time I had, and still have, a huge network of other business owners who specialise in different areas of maternal mental health and it's testament to the growing problem that so many of them were happy to provide thoughts, advice and ideas for the website. For some reason, going through pregnancy and giving birth seems to be the precursor to more and more of us experiencing anxiety long term.

One of the most supportive is the founder of the Guilt-Free Mum programme, Bindi Gauntlett. Bindi taught me a new word: matrescence. In fact, it's so new that the spell correct on my PC still gives it a red line underneath. You may know it as 'baby brain'. The problem being, that the term baby brain has become a bit of banter to lots of us and isn't really taken seriously. In fact, matrescence describes the physical, neurological and mental changes that a woman experiences when she goes through pregnancy and becomes a mum.

You can think of it in the same way we think about adolescence. During our teenage years, the way we are 'being', 'thinking', and 'feeling' changes from girl to adulthood. We experience the same changes from woman to motherhood. Fogginess, memory loss, difficulty with decision making, a roller coaster of emotions. We all experienced them as teenagers.

Pregnancy hormones, those which start labour, all work to change the way you think and the way that you feel. And on top of these hormones you also experience an increase in Cortisol and Oxytocin. The hormones for stress and love. We need these hormones to hold our babies close and look out for dangers. Our brains are on high alert for threats. The limbic system is a very primitive part of our brains which is there to keep us safe. It causes you to react rather than respond and is responsible for the fight or flight tendency.

We are all born with templates in our limbic systems, as you will know from the startle reflex in newborns when they throw their arms out. And as we go through life, we will lay down more of these templates. Things which will make us react, rather than respond. A lot of mums will become more scared of heights, going out after dark, or driving long distances once they have had children. Things that might have been second nature before.

What's important is that you realise this is the start of a new normal. Mummy brain is actually a real thing. A permanent change.

On the positive side, mums often find that their senses regarding what's going on around them are heightened, they're more able to multitask, they have an ability to keep going against all the odds (or after some seriously sleepless nights). They're driven to make the world a better place for themselves and their children. Recognising these newfound perspectives on life can really help with overcoming the anxiety-inducing downsides.

I won't walk along cliff tops anymore, I have worked out a plan if our car accidentally drives into a lake (my husband is responsible for getting the windows open, I look after the seat belts). I won't watch any crime documentaries involving children. And I have to check if the front door is locked twice every night. I write everything down and diarise my entire day, otherwise everything is completely forgotten about. But I can also work multiple, successful part-time jobs at once alongside running my own business. I get more done in a single day than I did in a whole week pre-kids. And thankfully I am still a fan of rollercoasters. A passion I have instilled in my daughter.

"Sometimes the strength of motherhood is greater than natural laws."

Barbara Kingsolver

HELEN SANDERS

Helen Sanders is one of the UK's leading hiring experts for business owner-led companies. She grew tired of working in an industry that is often tied to low/no morals and values, and recruitment consultants who seemingly don't care. Helen set up Your People Partners. The team partner (!) with business owners who need help growing their company and don't need traditional recruiters.

Helen's son, Leo, was aged 3 when diagnosed with cancer. A golf ball-sized tumour behind his right eye that needed immediate treatment. This happened just 4 days after Helen had a hysterectomy due to endometriosis.

Practicing the Pivot

It has taken me 42 attempts to sit here and write this.

To update our story… I need to get it on paper. Somehow, I need to sort through all these thoughts swirling around and access the ones I've pushed to a very dark part of my brain.

Yet something has stopped me each time.

Call it protecting myself.

Call it becoming overwhelmed.

Today, I woke up with absolute clarity about what I would like to share.

It all started with a beautiful blue-eyed boy with lovely blonde hair having a golf ball-sized brain. His name is Leo and he's three. He's my only child. The tumour was pushing his eyeball out of his head, yet he was fine! Leo was not off his food. No temperature. No discharge from his eye. He played with his Playmobil® with as much enthusiasm as usual.

In hindsight, the only difference (apart from the eyeball coming out of his head) was his energy levels were slightly off. I remember carrying him around a little as he was saying he was tired in the weeks leading up to diagnosis. The brain tumour was using the energy he had to enable its growth.

Bloody cancer, eh?

I asked, 'Is he going to die?'

'We don't know', the oncologist replied.

We needed to do everything we could to save him. Without urgent treatment, he would not be waking up in his room across from me as I type this. I was 33 when he was diagnosed. I had a hysterectomy four days before the cancer diagnosis. Here I was, thinking endometriosis was the worst thing my husband and I had dealt with, until that May bank holiday weekend in 2008 at the Bristol Children's Hospital.

So let's meander forward to the here and now, and boy, has parenting taken a different path for both my husband and me!

When we were expecting Leo, my husband, PJ, and I had aspirations and journeys we thought life would take us on. PJ was so excited about having a boy. He talked with much anticipation about dressing as superheroes and traipsing through Sainsbury's without a care in the world.

We talked with joy about Sunday bike rides, the three of us and a four-legged friend we'd yet to adopt. Like all new parents, you have a dream of a future that you think will come into fruition if you just steer towards and focus on what it is you want.

Okay, so our family life didn't entirely turn out to be all that.

I have the word 'pivot' in my head as I write this, and now a smile across my face as that word always reminds me of the Friends episode where they tried to get Ross's new couch up the stairs to his new apartment.

Our life pivoted in 2008, and I'd say we've got pretty good at pivoting (there's that knowing smile again).

In the last couple of years, my grief for the life we planned out together and the loss of our hopes have slowly but surely been replaced with many other utterly brilliant hopes and dreams. We've been on Disney holidays that would never have happened if things had been 'normal'. I would not be running my third company and so laser-focused on creating wealth for my family in the way I am.

Fear used to drive many of my decisions, but it is not something I live in anymore.

The question of, 'What happens if something happens to Leo and we've not given him a joyful, full life?', has been resolved.

With each year that passes, we're lucky enough to still be the three of us. Well, actually, the four of us, after our fabulous cocker spaniel, Bubba, came into our family in 2013. We thought he would be good therapy for

Leo. It turns out our Bubba provides a very individual therapeutic service to each of us. He just seems to know what each of us needs and when we need it. Such a special dog, and I'm confident he makes me a better parent too!

How do I bridge the story of our parenting between 2008 and today?

It's safe to say that many of the, 'If he survives, he'll end up with X, Y and Z' has come true.

Learning disabilities.

Cataracts.

Secondary cataracts.

Panhypopituitary axis problems – his body parts work, but his brain doesn't tell 'them' to. For example: he has problems with his thyroid and requires growth hormone injections daily.

M.E. Bloody M.E. Reducing sight in both eyes with right eye considerably yucky and pretty much redundant now.

And more…

Leo didn't get any GCSEs.

However, unlike the mother I thought I'd be when we first had Leo, I am not disappointed about this. We learned far more important things than what he couldn't learn due to his learning disabilities.

Having to shield for months upon end from a virus he thought would kill him was the focus for a while. We didn't know for a long time that at the same time as we had the shielding letter through the door, he'd received a text directly from the NHS. The text linked to the first shielding letter sent out in March 2020.

If you've ever read that letter, you'll know that the intentions were good. All the NHS was doing was trying to protect people they felt were highly vulnerable at a time of great uncertainty. For a 15-year-old who is intelligent yet struggles with nuance, the language and phrases used in the letter led to many months of poor mental health. I am writing this in April 2022, and he still isn't getting out of the house most days.

Parenting a bright child that doesn't fit the norms has been extraordinarily challenging yet wildly rewarding.

Before the pandemic, when he was well enough, he'd attended a special school for brilliant kids with learning disabilities. What we've become accustomed to as parents is being an advocate for our child, something we wish he had never needed. Even getting him into a school that could help him took over £10k put on a credit card to pay for a lawyer to fight his corner. No parent should have to foot that bill, with the credit card interest, it'll likely amount to over £20k before it's paid off.

No parenting book or website will tell you just how neurotic you'll (have to) come across as when defending your child, especially when they don't fit into a box.

Indeed, a local authority educational psychologist (ed-psych) once told the headteacher at his primary school that they'd never heard of radiotherapy damaging a child's brain, and to just appease the mum as needed.

I'm still astounded at this ed psych's lack of professionalism here. Indeed, I could have introduced them to Leo's oncologists, and they'd have provided all the evidence they needed. Irradiate a child's brain at the age of 3, and if they survive, they're in for life-limitations and some significant physical and mental deficits.

Thankfully another ed-psych said to us that we would not have a traditional academic life with Leo. However, they also said that he is exceptionally smart. That is all we needed to give us the push as we continued to navigate each pivot (and there's that smile across my face again!).

When he wasn't well enough for school, Leo taught himself how to animate and create videos. His YouTube channel has over 1000 subscribers, and he didn't let us, his parents, help him in this pursuit or learning journey.

He couldn't tell the time, and we needed to reteach him simple maths every day; however, he was teaching himself highly technical things that most people cannot even try to achieve. The bits of his brain that are damaged by radiotherapy have started to rewire, and the bits that were not damaged, I feel they just got enhanced. Surely that makes him superhuman?

We have the same stubborn boy we had at age three.

This is why he's alive.

He's now 17, and we still don't know what the future holds. We don't know what 18, 19, or his 20's, will look like for him and that does not matter at all.

It is the here and now that counts.

I've come to learn and accept my role as his parent and advocate. I will ensure he is a happy 17 year old, then a happy 18 year old. Everything else is secondary to his happiness.

My goal for him now is to ensure he gets the mental health support he needs: introduce and explore with him new adventures that may or may not light his fire, continue to see family outside the house as he feels able, head to the movies as often as feels able and perhaps even see a few old friends from school more than once every 3-6 months.

Our goals in 2023 may be a little different.

As a parent, I hope so, as life will continue to evolve and change.

However, I won't be upset if we've only made tiny steps in a few of these current goals. I will continue to ensure he gets the support he wants and needs, and I will never get upset or frustrated when there are steps back. It's an exhausting way to live and has had an awful impact on my own mental and general health. Only at the start of this year did I understand that I cannot be at my best for him unless I am well, of mind and body.

Over the years, I've done different things to look after myself. However, as a parent who used to put Leo's oxygen mask on first at all times, I now know that unless my mask is firmly in place I cannot be at my best and healthiest for him.

The 'me' of a few years back would ask if he is going to live.

The 'me' of now says, he's here, he's very much alive.

He has the sharpest wit and is very talented.

He has been able to teach himself skills he'd never have learned in school.

We do what we can to support and guide Leo to be the happiest he can be. His mental health is more important than whether he has a degree or lives independently. This may all sound obvious, however, I am confident that I would have been a very different parent: mapping out his life based on my expectations.

This is the lesson of the cancer journey I've learned: life is about being well in mind and body.

That includes being able to cope when life pivots.

Leo has two parents, and this update is only my take on this life of parenting. PJ and I are still married. We've found our individual roles in how we contribute to Leo's parenting needs.

I appreciate that many families don't stay together when there is such chronic illness and challenges. Having our incredible boy has taught us so much. It has enabled our marriage to be flexible and to be what we need as a couple, and also provide Leo with a loving environment.

I am acknowledging in writing that I am grateful for having not had more children.

I am also acknowledging to the universe that I love my life.

Parenting is a journey, and I will continue to pivot with it.

I am happy.

So is Leo (at times).

We'll keep going to ensure more happiness in his days, weeks, months and years.

Life is here.

We'll continue to live it!

"Mother Nature is providential. She gives us twelve years to develop a love for our children before turning them into teenagers."

William Galvin

JO DAVIES

Joanna lives with her husband and three children in Gloucestershire, juggling life as a busy mum, work as a leadership and resilience coach, an interiors blogger and Zumba instructor.

Jo spent twenty five years working in the arts and cultural industries as a marketing and branding specialist, and five years ago changed direction to work as a Lay Member in the governance of the NHS in Gloucestershire whilst completing an MSc in Strategy, Change and Leadership, alongside professional coaching certifications. She now works with clients in developing their personal brand, building resilience (particularly following a long absence from work following ill health) and leadership development. She uses creative writing and brand development techniques to help clients to find their purpose and drive, be clear on who they are and what values underpin their work.

Connect with Jo:
Email: joanna@theclarityhub.co.uk
Website: www.theclarityhub.co.uk
LinkedIn: www.linkedin.com/company/the-clarity-hub

The Truth, the Whole Truth and Nothing Less About My Butt

What shall we tell them?

That was pretty much all that was at the forefront of our minds when it happened. We'd seen the consultant surgeon and been told that I had rectal cancer; a large tumour, but no other details at that stage. We'd been told that there would be more tests, scans, and that after that they would confirm the stage of cancer and the treatment plan. But they were pretty sure it was cancer.

At the time our children were seven, eight and ten. They were bright, happy and (we hoped) resilient. I wanted to tell them the truth, but my husband wasn't sure. He didn't want to frighten them, not until we knew for sure. As it turned out it would be several weeks before we found out the extent of what was about to come, and I didn't want to keep it from them for any amount of time, as that felt like lying to them. I argued that if we lied to them now, they wouldn't trust us when they really needed to. I was sure they would overhear whispered conversations, sense something was wrong, or see concern on our faces. I also didn't want everyone else in the family to know while they didn't, as there was always the potential for someone to let something slip. So we sat them down that evening. 'I've been for some tests.' I told them, 'And I've got to have some more but I've definitely got to have an operation'. I paused to let that bit sink in, but before I could continue our eldest asked, 'Is it cancer?'. What could I say to that? Lie? Fudge about a bit? Blurt it out without preparing the ground first? Instead I simply said: 'Possibly, yes. We don't know for sure but yes, it might be.'

And then it came. 'Are you going to be alright?'

What to say next?

'Yes, of course!'

But I might not be. We had no idea at that stage how bad it would be, what treatment I might have, or indeed whether it had spread. I had ignored the symptoms for 6 months, put it down to age, menopause or stress. So it could be bad. It could be everywhere. The children at that time had already been faced with cancer, two of them had best friends whose mothers had had breast cancer, and both had recovered post treatment. Their grandad had been treated for cancer and was fine. Another friend had received treatment for three different, unrelated cancers and was as fit as a fiddle. I took a deep breath and said: 'I don't know, but we hope so.' and talked about everyone they knew who had been diagnosed with cancer and got better. And that was that. They took the news, hugged me and carried on with their evening, and we breathed a sigh of relief that they knew as much as we knew and sat back to contemplate what might come next.

What did come next was an 18 month period of treatment of radiotherapy, major surgery to remove 'Keith' (the tumour's nickname!), an ileostomy bag to allow my colon to heal, an awful post op infection (one silver lining – two and a half stone lost in five weeks. Result!), 7 months of chemo, sepsis and then the reversal op. All of which was squeezed in amidst the global pandemic that would see everyone joining us in isolation and a sense of stasis. From the beginning I had been adamant that I wanted to use language that the children would understand, but that was also truthful. The word cancer was used a lot. I believed then and I believe it more now that we shouldn't let the word be terrifying, so we never shied away from it. Cancer, cancer, cancer. I have no idea whether it was the right thing to do, but when (not if, the stats tell us that) they encounter cancer again in the future, hopefully the word will not strike terror in their hearts. In a similar vein of thought, other language was banned. No-one was permitted to talk about me 'battling' cancer, fighting it or aiming to be a 'survivor'. No-one was to tell me (or them) I was on a journey, tilt their head to one side and look at me with sympathetic eyes, or mutter in hushed tones about how brave I was being. I was ill, I was being treated, and hopefully I would get better. I never wanted them to think that if I didn't get better, I hadn't battled enough, hadn't fought to stay with them. Because that really was what it was all about from that first day – I would take whatever treatment I had to, just to stay with them.

The children, for their part, accepted what they were told and got on with their lives. In novels, children who are going through a difficult time rise to the occasion, become angels, mopping fevered brows and take on household chores at the same time as winning vast scholarships to elite schools. No such thing happened in our household. Our 12-year-old daughter made the most of her raging hormones with door slamming, shouting fits, tears and possessing the startling ability to completely forget that I had just undergone 4 hours of chemo. Our angel of a son gradually turned into a morose stinker, obsessed with the PlayStation, while our baby girl turned from a small 7-year-old to a 9-year-old football playing whirlwind in the blink of an eye. We had been determined that they would not miss out on childhood adventures just because I couldn't go, so there were times when I lay in bed simultaneously laughing at the photos sent to me of them at a family festival, or at the Regent's Park Open Air Theatre, and crying because I wasn't with them. Their friends were always welcome for playdates and sleepovers and became used to me lying in bed looking ill. Some arrived with get well soon cards, and always offered hugs. I would lie in bed watching them in the garden, laughing and kicking a football around, or listen to them giggling in bed at night, and congratulate myself on the fact that what was happening was doing them absolutely no harm at all. But looking back on it now, there are things that break my heart.

It is strange to say but when the day of my first operation dawned, there was a sense of excitement in the house. They'd made cards and painted stones for me, helped me pack my bag and chose magazines for me to take. As I waved them off to school that morning, they all told me they loved me. They still don't know that I wrote them letters in case I didn't wake up (during all of it, the anaesthetic is what scared me most), letters that told them how much I loved them, how proud I am of who they are and how they treat others. If they had known how scared I was, how would that have affected them? Maybe they did know. The hugs that morning certainly were tight. And when they came to see me in hospital they all showed their struggles in their own ways. My son was fighting so hard to hide how much hospitals scared him. My daughter chatted away to the other patients on the ward so that she didn't have to look at the tubes, the drains, the ileostomy bag, the worn out, thin, pale mother in the tired, dishevelled looking bed. A thought that still hurts was when my lovely, kind daughter was being bullied at secondary school, I was too worn out with the onslaught of chemotherapy drugs to leap to her defence and she had to deal with it on her own. These memories do not fade and are accompanied by a deep sense of guilt.

And what of their dad? In one of those fantastic alignments of ill fate, he had been made redundant the week after my diagnosis. And then suddenly he was mother, father, taxi driver, holiday planner, job seeker and more. All the usual parenting trials and tribulations like accidents (and trips to A&E!), birthdays, homework, visits to the optician, they don't stop simply because one parent has cancer. So he was sitting by my bedside on an acute ward, getting home at 2.30a.m. and having to get up early the next morning to sort packed lunches and football kits. But he did it. We did it, and of course, they did it.

So what did I learn through our 18 months of upheaval? First and foremost is that the most important thing I ever taught my children was resilience. When we emerged from chemo, prepared to kickstart our normal life again, we had just 3 weeks before the whole nation was told to lock down. Where many children suffered anxiety through the pandemic, mine appeared to sail through it. They had already learned to be flexible, to take each day as it came and to rely on each other and those around them for comfort and support. They had built skills whilst I was ill, and can cook for themselves, do the washing and clean the house (they CAN, doesn't mean they DO!). I now know that I can send them off into the world prepared to meet adversity head on, and to talk honestly about how they are dealing with it. We learned that family is so much more than you might think and that 'parenting' happens in many ways. When one of my closest friends had been diagnosed with breast cancer, and we discussed the impact on her girls, I remember her telling me that they were so lucky, because they had five mums, me included. I later found this to be so true for us, when we were told to get me to hospital sharpish, not to wait for the ambulance, and my friends stepped up to scoop up my babies, feed them, love them and make them feel safe. My children too have many 'mothers' and know that they have a network of parents around them who will always be there for them. And honesty. We told the truth, and they coped. They are not scared of the word 'cancer' and for that I am grateful. I believe it will prove valuable in the years ahead.

I wonder sometimes whether cancer has changed me, changed us, and changed the way we are as a family. I think the truthful answer is yes, of course it has. I worry more now about them being left on their own, of something happening to my husband and me, and how we can make sure they're safe and brought up in the way we would wish for them. I worry even more about something happening to them – illness, injury, pain of any kind. I know now that I can't protect them from everything, and that my previous feeling of invincibility was a fallacy. But I don't think it's changed the way we parent. We still approach that head on, up front, with sometimes alarming frankness. That's how we tackled parenting through cancer, and we got through it, and I suppose only time will tell whether it has affected the children more deeply than we know. In a way it readied us for what was to come during the pandemic, but has it prepared us in any way for exams, leaving home, relationship break ups or our children's own parenting approach? Maybe. We know honesty works, protects them, and builds trust. I can only hope they will take that lesson forward with them, and that they know they can tell us the truth no matter what and we will face the consequences together. I'm not saying I'm glad I had cancer, that my husband had to watch me be so ill whilst having to work so hard to keep a focus on the children and their lives, their fears, their everyday happenings, but neither do I see it as being a terribly damaging period in our lives. We laughed our way through it. Mostly about farting, but still, we did it together.

"Your children are not your children, they come through you, but they are life itself, wanting to express itself."

Wayne Dyer

LEIGH CROFT

Leigh lives in Gloucestershire with her family, cockapoo and medley of small furries.

She has run her own training and development business for the last 20 years and in the last few years has switched her focus to 1:1 coaching with corporate and non-corporate clients. Her focus is working with clients who feel 'stuck' and have a desire to shift patterns and behaviours which are hindering them in being who they truly want to be.

Starting as a psychologist, she has pursued her personal/career development as an NLP Master Practitioner, and an mBIT certified coach, building skill and expertise as a coach.

She loves baking and cooking, running and the gym and supporting her kids with their many sporting activities, walking the dog and catching up with friends.

Connect with Leigh:

Email: leigh@theclarityhub.co.uk and leigh@training4fusion.co.uk

Website: www.theclarityhub.co.uk and www.training4fusion.co.uk

LinkedIn: www.linkedin.com/company/the-clarity-hub

Learning to Thrive When Your Husband Falls Off the Reality Shelf

So what compelled me to write this – a chapter in my life that brought me to my knees emotionally? Or more accurately, curled up under the kitchen table clutching a bottle of wine like it was a lifeline while I sobbed and hoped the world would be different when I emerged.

I look back and still wonder what did I do to get a double dose of chaos while everyone else got the prescribed pandemic and home-schooling – which quite frankly should be enough in anyone's book!

Simultaneously my business collapsed, due to the pandemic, and I became a single parent to my three gorgeous kids, a pooch, two guinea pigs, two rats and a bearded dragon. My husband and partner of 24 years had a mental breakdown and buggered off for 18 months on a sabbatical from life. His mission appeared to be to cause as much havoc and destruction to his life as was inhumanly possible! Me and the kids were simply the collateral damage.

So this is really about single parenting through 18 months of uncertainty and isolation, while trying to guess the next moves of a hugely clever man who lost his reality lens on the world. He embarked on a solo adventure of world domination and destruction, all the while either forgetting that he had a family or pretending to. A decision that was hurtful, destructive and dismissive, that left our family scarred.

It started gradually; small, quirky, behavioural changes that caused me to look sideways at him and wonder what was going on. He stopped sleeping, drank massive amounts of caffeine, and wasn't able to open his mouth without a stream of swear words erupting (nasty ones too). He began smoking excessively, condemning the household to high volume rock music at 7a.m., and storming out of the house if he was challenged. Often coming back hours or days later.

He had previously experienced depression and taken anti-depressants, but this was different. He got a buzz out of lying and knowing that I knew he was lying. His extreme level of paranoia meant that he secretly recorded conversations as evidence to later fling back at me. He was secretive, aggressive, and taking risks, financially, socially and in everything he did.

The final straw for me was when he stormed out after triggering an argument and strutted in the next morning, clutching a take-out coffee, claiming he was too tired to take his son to rugby – and went to bed.

I had been on the phone to the police, the hospitals and had been worried sick, but I put a brave face on and went to rugby, because that's what mums do. Then I asked him to move out for a few days and think about his behaviour. After that I was solo. He hardly came back and seemed to have no empathy for me or the children and didn't seem to care about the impact of his behaviour.

So, what could I tell the kids? It was clear to them Daddy had changed – the house had shifted from calm and happy to stressed and loud. There was a sense of relief in the house when he went, but also we worried he might come back.

I couldn't hide my emotions – we were together 24/7 due to lockdown, so I was as honest as I could be. Some things I didn't share, like police calls trying to locate him after traffic accidents, drink driving offences, and his suicide threats. I did tell them that Daddy wasn't very well and that I suspected, having educated myself through the wonders of Google, that he was likely bipolar. He just seemed to be experiencing the 'manic' side, where he thought he was above rules and ultimately right in everything he did. I've since adopted my own term: 'multi-polar' – it's 3D, spiralling and cycles too quickly to identify lows, just manic, manic, manic…

I'm human so as much as I tried to shield the children from his actions,

I couldn't always hide my anger at his behaviour on a few occasions. For example when he stole my van from the driveway, because he had crashed his car into a field and written it off. He could have walked back to his home quicker but for some reason he felt he had a right to take my car. I woke up in an absolute panic as I was due to take the children to Cornwall the following day.

He climbed through my third storey window to access a plug socket to resurface my driveway while I was away. Imagine my 18-year-old house sitters' horror when she woke up to find the window wide open and the key vanished from the inside lock so she couldn't secure the house – she thought she was going mad!

And then he threatened to expose me in the local paper (I was most disgruntled he didn't think I warranted at least a Sunday tabloid) for adultery and general nastiness if I didn't give him our beloved family dog.

At that point I told the children I was divorcing Daddy – not because he didn't love them, but because he wasn't very well and he didn't want any help to get better. I always told them that one day Daddy would get better and maybe be able to be a dad again. My ultimate fear throughout this whole time was that he would kill himself or someone else and leave a very different legacy for my children to deal with.

The children and I became a very tight unit – we talked, we shared fears and worries, and I regularly checked in on how they were feeling about their dad – did they want to see him? The answer seemed to be a resounding yes, but only if he is better!

If we did see him, generally it was a disaster. He whispered to them that mummy was ill and was poisoning them against him. Although it broke my heart, I realised the current dynamics were too unhealthy to expose the children to. It must have been really hard for them to understand his behaviour – I couldn't get my head around it – it was like an alien had inhabited his body and wiped out any love, compassion or relationship with his family. It was probably hardest for my 13-year-old as he could see the challenge I was facing. It was hard to hide both, how I was emotionally coping with the alien abduction of my husband and my desperate attempts to get the overstretched NHS to first, acknowledge him and then make him better. The harsh reality is that they can only help if someone wants help, unless the person is a risk to themselves or others. Although he was a risk, he was clever enough to imply that I was just a bitter wife out to get him and he was a highly successful entrepreneur.

My 13-year-old became the man of the house and was very defensive of me. He helped with the bins, with his little brother and walking the dog. My daughter was desperate for Daddy to be better and regularly wanted to see him. She wanted to explore what his state was. This was tricky to manage, she wanted to see for herself while I wanted to protect her from being rejected again!

My youngest was most confused, he hated home-schooling. At age 7 he really couldn't see why he should do schoolwork at home and certainly not with me helping him. In the end we called a truce – he did the bare minimum and I didn't make him write stories – for some reason writing fiction at home was enough to reduce both of us to tears of frustration. My mum and dad video called every day so he could read to them and we muddled by.

The one positive I take from the whole experience is that the bond I have with my children is super strength – nothing is going to break it. We were vulnerable, scared and brave together, so we created little bedtime rituals that are just between the four of us and we know that whatever happens we won't let each other down!

That's something their dad lost and may never regain, the unconditional trust of a child is a beautiful thing, but once it is lost there are no guarantees it will come back.

Through it all I did my best as a parent. The kids ate healthy food, we did stuff together, went on adventures and holidays, played games, had duvet days and watched back-to-back movies on the sofa with pizza and cake. I kept talking to them and explaining, your dad loves you – he just can't show it right now.

The thing that kept me from crawling under the table and opening that bottle of wine was my parents' unwavering support and our circle of five.

My dad became a role model for the kids on what a man can be like and went out of his way to support my prepubescent manchild who had a lot of anger and hurt swirling around his system. They say the role of a parent never ends and you never stop worrying about your children. I suspect my situation turned my parents' hair white on many occasions. My dad coached me back into singleton independence – changing the locks (which strangely felt like betrayal), filing for divorce and to keep going when my husband insisted in long rambling letters (which cost me a fortune for my solicitor to read) that there was nothing wrong with our marriage and we weren't getting divorced.

My mum is a star, when I was full of rage and anger, she always reminded me that my husband was ill and that he didn't realise he was behaving that way. She still insisted I divorce him before he took me and the children down with him financially and emotionally!

I had a circle of friends who allowed me to rant, vouched for my sanity and listened to me go round in circles during the really tough times. Every parent needs this circle and it needs to be yours – not shared with your partner.

So, what did I learn from this gruesome and grisly experience? What pearls of wisdom can I share that might help you if you were to end up in a similar scenario?

Sometimes you have to listen to your heart, but obey your head. If someone is toxic and destructive to you and your children, no matter how much you love them or what history you share, you can't stay. It's a tough lesson and I lost a lot of weight grappling between the emotions of loyalty and love versus preservation and cold hard survival.

Take life one second, one minute at a time – just get through the next hour if that is what's needed. You will get there.

Ask for help. It's ok to show you are vulnerable – there is a time to be strong and a time to accept everything that is offered, lifts to school, to football, supper- just grab it by the balls and say thank you!

Some people just won't get it, so don't waste precious energy trying to explain it to them. Focus on your circle – people who get you, get the situation and have your best interests at heart!

When mental illness affects an individual, it affects the whole family – sometimes the family suffer more when the ill person has lost touch with reality and doesn't have a clue how destructive they are being.

Above all – breathe in for six and out for six as often as you can – it balances out your autonomic nervous system and brings balance so you can step out of fight and flight response, even if only temporarily.

One day the alien left, leaving a damaged, shell-shocked man wondering how he had believed he'd been so right! My husband found his way back to the reality shelf, sought help and is building a new life with me and his children. It won't be the same, not for the children and certainly not for me. I'm not the same person, I have boundaries and independence – and he isn't the same either. But I have learnt that I have more compassion and forgiveness than I thought possible. And I think that's a really good trait to role model for children. People do deserve second chances, mental illness can happen to any of us.

"I realized when you look at your mother, you are looking at the purest love you will ever know."

Mitch Albom

LIZ WALTON

I'm Liz, who thought she could do anything… until I couldn't.

As a therapist, I unlocked the innate healing within my clients. My life was perfect, until a shock-wave hit…

After ten years trying to conceive and £30,000 of unsuccessful IVF, my emotions and my marriage were in tatters.

After healing *myself*, I became precariously pregnant with a baby unlikely to survive.

This unborn child now demanded my complete and utter surrender to her life or death.

Only when I accepted her terms did Willow stay to be born. I was 46.

Now I help others on their fertility journey.

Connect with Liz:

Website: www.lizwalton.org

Facebook: www.facebook.com/LizWaltonfertilitycoach/

Instagram: @Lizwalton_fertilitycoach

So What Happens After the Impossible is Created?

Well, in fact, life does carry on.

It's interesting how life is all about cycles and the 'hows' – how we learn, how we deal with things, how we grow, how we get back up and how we start all over again.

It's been interesting re-reading the chapter I wrote before my journey with fertility and it was beautiful reading it knowing that, at that point, I had 3 weeks to go before I had my baby.

What I'd like to share with you is that 46-year-old woman (me) really did have a wonderful birthing experience. I did my utmost to create the best birth that I could possibly have. I didn't listen to any negative stories of births, even though there seems to be a lot of horrible stories around. I made sure I just watched the best births possible like orgasmic births and hypnobirths. I just filled my body, my mind and my senses with all of this possibility.

I chanted and om'd my beautiful baby out. I did have an amazing Doula; I highly recommend having one. She was amazing at helping me birth my daughter and was superb at guiding myself and my husband because it can be quite a daunting experience having a baby.

I found becoming a mother to be such a breathtaking experience. We don't necessarily know how to do it and yet there's a part of us, this primal, ancient part that does. I remember saying my daughter is new at this baby thing and I am new at this mother thing and together we will slowly work it out. And I feel that's kind of what we did. And it's not always easy, evidenced by the plenty of crying by me and the new baby. But I think the biggest discovery was the amount of remarkable, all-encompassing, unadulterated love I had for my baby, Willow. Being around her I couldn't stop looking into her eyes or kissing her constantly. This love that I had never experienced in my life was all pervading. And it was intoxicating. Which is just as well because this parenthood thing is quite tiring.

For the first year of my baby's life, I was also caring for my exceptionally elderly mother. This was very challenging as I was a new, but older mother, and my own mother was obviously on her way to her next phase of existence. This was very bittersweet, very emotional and at times very difficult, and yet it was beautiful. I cherish those times and, luckily, I have lots of beautiful pictures of my mom with my daughter in that first year of her life.

After my dear mother passed away, we took a year to sort everything out before we went back to Australia. In Australia we set up a new life and settled into a new way of being.

As Willow got older, the relationship got more interesting. No longer could I just put her in clothes and sit her down or tell her what to do, she was beginning to learn she could say no. What do you do when a child says no? What is the best way to connect and communicate with your child?

For me, these questions put me on another path of wanting to learn. To understand, to communicate and be as conscious as I could with parenting. I needed to cultivate my own parenting skills because I wanted to learn a new way to parent. It's true in a lot of ways that you'll end up parenting in a similar way to your parents' style, but I also think each generation needs to be able to update and grow with the next stages and era of parenting.

I set out to find answers to my questions of how to learn and communicate with my child, and I discovered the answers and much more.

I found courses, one was called Parent Effectiveness Training or PET. This was awesome and I highly recommend this to any new parents or parents of any kind.

I got into lots of different podcasts, one is the 'Good Enough Mother' by Dr. Sophie Brooke. An astonishingly good look at what it means to be a mom, how we get there and all the thoughts and things that can happen. She does a brilliant job and I thoroughly recommend it.

Another podcast which I follow all the time is 'Nourishing the Mother'. Two amazing women created this great vessel of discussion of what it means to parent, covering everything from how do we do that for our kids, to being a conscious parent and holding the space for kids to feel. Again, a phenomenal podcast that I highly recommend.

I also researched schools and different philosophies and became interested in the values of the Steiner School. Look up Lou Zarah Harvey, she is amazing and I have had several parenting one-on -ones with her on how I can parent. Her book and Facebook page are called 'Happy Child, Happy Home'. I have learnt so much from her about parenting with nature.

I was also lucky enough to meet a beautiful woman called Joanne Holbrook, who while she was living here in Canberra, Australia wrote a book called 'Passport to Parenting' (in book form and on Audible). She had brought up two children whilst living all over the world because her husband was in the American Army. Her tips, her thoughts and her ideas have flowed with my values and informed my own ways of parenting.

I'm about to write a book about my fertility journey and my healing, not just from fertility but my life. I know one of my chapters will be starting with the saying, 'when the student is ready, the teacher will appear'. Willow is really one of my biggest teachers. She teaches me about time, she teaches me to stop and she teaches me to enjoy the little things. She teaches me to laugh and play and to stop rushing. I never knew that having a child would mean that she would become one of my biggest teachers. That was something I never thought about on my fertility journey.

One of my main learnings as I reflect, and one I talk alot about with clients, is that huge question, 'Why me? Why do I have to be the one with a fertility journey? Why do I have all this pain? What's wrong with me?'

I now know this is the best time to turn this conversation around!

I have translated this into 'Well, why not you?'

I feel the fertility journey is a calling. A calling for any individual to be more. More than they have ever realised they could be. A fertility journey gives us the opportunity: you, my clients and myself, to be stripped down to our cores. To be laid bare along with everything that we thought was real, our values and beliefs, all being questioned. The wonderful thing about that is when there's nothing left we can be rebuilt into a new version of us. A version with more compassion, more love and more understanding and healing. Through this we can become the best versions of who we are; more resilient, stronger and more aware. We have to be more, to be the best versions of ourselves to create the next generation, because the next generation needs to change this world for the better.

So what this means is that for anyone on a fertility journey, this is the calling for you to go deeper, to search and go deep into your soul. It's time for you to heal every aspect of your life, so that you become a blank canvas. None of this stuff has to be handed down to this little being that will come into your life; they can grow up to be well balanced and well adjusted. Through this, we can help this beautiful world in all of its goodness and its badness, and shape it because these new beings are needed to save our planet. And this is how a fertility journey becomes one of the most amazing things we will ever do. Remember the fertility journey is really a gift.

I continue to learn to be a better parent, in fact I love learning and I love how Willow teaches me every day. I feel very blessed that I have been given this opportunity. I must admit I do fall down a lot. I do think I could do it better and I could be a better parent, a better person and better role model.

I think we all feel sometimes that we could do better, so I do the best I can and the best I can is good enough. It's me learning every day.

So watch this space and let's see how both myself and Willow progress.

My last message to you is to fully enjoy the life you've got, because you really are the treasure worth finding. When you find that treasure so many other things can fall into place.

With all our love, Liz and Willow.

"One child, one teacher, one book, one pen can change the world."

Malala Yousafzai

MARIA NEWMAN

Maria Newman is otherwise known as Mummy on a Break. She is the founder of The Busy Working Mums Club, is a coach, mentor and trainer.

Having been on her own journey to become unstuck, Maria now helps ambitious mums overcome their challenges so they can lead a happy and calm life whilst being a great role model through 1:1 coaching.

Maria grew up in the West Country and now lives in Bristol with her husband and two children.

Maria has many passions in life that support her well-being. She believes that anything can be solved by sitting around the dinner table and eating a delicious meal that she's cooked. She loves being outside and going for a run, not necessarily because she loves running but because she gets time to herself, she gets to listen to an inspiring book on Audible and she can immerse herself in nature. She also enjoys the discipline and physical challenge of kickboxing martial arts, which started because she won a freebie in a Christmas raffle in 2018.

To find out more, come and connect with Maria:

Website: www.mummyonabreak.co.uk

Facebook group: www.facebook.com/groups/thebusyworkingmumsclub

Facebook page: www.facebook.com/MummyOnABreak

Instagram: @mummyonabreak

LinkedIn: www.linkedin.com/in/maria-newman/

Podcast: www.anchor.fm/mummyonabreak

Pinterest: www.pinterest.co.uk/mummyonabreakMaria/

YouTube: www.youtube.com/channel/UClEhv_9PngF-jQHiuBI1pkg

You Don't Have to Do the Mummy Juggle

Being a mum is hard. Being a parent is hard. Even when you think all is going well it can feel like it's still going wrong, or it isn't quite right or you could have done it better. But the biggest thing I've learnt is the world doesn't need to stop just because you have children. You don't need to put your life on hold. Life is just different.

Just like water that flows freely down a river, adapting as it goes, becoming a mum is our opportunity to adapt to a new way of living. It can be that simple but it does take practice.

One of the most important lessons I've learnt is, life is not about sacrificing your hopes and dreams until your children have spread their wings and flown the nest. It's about being the best role model you can be to them. Showing them that you can lead a fulfilled life whilst still being the best mum you can be.

I'm an ordinary mum, just like you, just trying to live my best life. I know that sounds like a cliché but it's true. But to do this, I have to put myself first occasionally. Do what I want as well.

For life to work for me, I'm practicing balancing.

I see life as a constant balancing act. There is no such thing as achieving balance. I've tried to get there, many times. It's just not possible as we cannot control everything. We only really have control of ourselves. What we think, what we say and how we behave.

We know that there will be times during our lives, that the odd curveball will come our way. Our plans will not always work out how we expected them to. People will not always support us in the way we expected them to. I accept that life will sometimes feel unfair.

However, it's our ability to respond to the curveballs which will determine whether we survive and thrive or get stuck and start to sink.

When I first became a mum, I started to take life a lot more seriously. I had been given a gift. A massive responsibility. What I saw, was a perfectly packaged bundle of love. My Lea. There was no way I was going to mess this up. I was going to be the best I could be. She would have my complete attention. I'd become rigid in my thinking.

I thought it was all on me!

That's when I started to lose myself.

That's when I started running on the treadmill of life. Going through the same routine every day, to the point that I felt like I was just going through the motions. I had demoted myself to the bottom of my list.

Every day would end the same way, with me sitting exhausted on the sofa. I had no energy to do anything other than watch television until it was time for bed. I was sinking and I didn't even know it.

Whereas it seemed different for my husband. He wasn't exhausted. He seemed to be having more fun. Enjoying life.

The thing is, he was working just as hard as me and having fun. Why was I missing out on having fun?

With hindsight, I can now say it was because he was focused on having fun instead of the 101 things that I, and most mums, focus on before the fun can happen! Because that's what happens when you become a mum.

When I first became a mum, my main focus was on ensuring that I kept my baby safe. Was she dressed appropriately? Was I feeding her enough? Was her environment safe? I was a worrier. I was her protector. If anything bad happened to her, it would be my fault.

Whereas my husband was more relaxed. He had the same concerns but he seemed to be enjoying having her in our life. He was balancing.

This didn't really change when we had our son. In fact, I probably got a little worse, especially when he caught bronchiolitis, which meant a week's stay in the hospital when he was just 3 weeks old. I've never been so scared of losing someone so precious. I really thought this was it. Game over.

But over time, I realised that if I wanted things to change, if I wanted to have fun with my children, I needed to change. Not so easy when you're a project manager, a professional organiser!

I've learnt it's a matter of perspective. It's a matter of priority. It's a matter of what's important.

Just because he's Fun Dad doesn't mean you can't be Fun Mum.

It's all about choice. We are in control of what we think, say and do. So being Fun Mum is all about changing the way we think, what we say and what we do.

Here are 5 things to think about that will get you started.

Importance

Decide what is important to you. Obviously, there are chores that need to be done, some of which are important. But not everything that we fill our day with is important. Plus we really don't have to do everything ourselves. We do have options. We can ask for help.

Prioritise

If you know what is important you can then decide what is your priority. This may sound clinical but it really isn't. If you want to have fun, then it has to be your priority. As long as you know your children are clothed and fed, the rest can wait.

Top tip, agree on some boundaries as a family so that everyone has time to do their 'boring stuff'.

Focus on One Thing

Men are better at this than us women. We insist on juggling, which as I've said before, is a waste of effort. Being a fun mum is much easier if you're fully present with your children, rather than trying to multi task!

Judgement

We worry too much about what everyone else thinks rather than what we think. We know what is best for ourselves and our family and that's what matters. It's about trusting your instinct rather than dwelling on what is right or wrong according to Freda the Supermum!

Go With the Flow

Let it go and go with the flow. I love a plan and routine, but having fun cannot be planned or scheduled. It happens when you dare to let go. To just go with whatever is happening, without the drama of organising and making sure everything is just so.

My children are now 9 and 6 years old, so I am better at letting go and relaxing a little. But I've been practicing, a lot, and I'll continue to practice because I want to enjoy life.

The times I find myself reverting back to busy mum, mum with little time and not in the mood for fun, is when I'm trying to do too much. When I'm trying to do everything.

As I've said, being able to live life to its fullest is about balancing. And that's why it's about focusing on what's really important, rather than what needs to be done. It's so much easier, trust me.

As a mum, we wear lots of different hats. We take on a lot of different roles. But I want you to realise that you are more than the roles you play in your life. I want you to be able to reacquaint yourself with who you really are. Remember the things you enjoyed doing before you became a mum.

I want you to accept that it's okay to put yourself first. You too deserve to have your wants and needs met, without putting your life on hold whilst you support those who you love.

I want you to remember what's important to you. What really matters to you. Who really matters to you. Where you want to focus your energy.

I want you to be able to believe in yourself so that you can get what you want because you do deserve to have whatever you want and there is plenty to go around. It's not selfish, there's no need to feel guilty and it's not greedy.

I want you to be comfortable with being the lead actor in your life. There is no need to be the observer in your life. Only you can be the lead actor, which doesn't mean being loud. It means having the courage to decide what's best for you and then do it.

I want you to embrace your ability to dream. To see in colour what you want to happen before it happens in reality. Because if you know where you're going it will be so much easier to get there.

As mums, we can choose to live in the shadow of mum guilt. Thinking we're being selfish if we put ourselves first. Thinking we're not good enough. Thinking we're not doing our best. But it doesn't have to be this way.

I would like you to give yourself permission to step out of the shadows and know it is okay to be you. Because you are good enough. Because you always do your best. And because putting yourself first is necessary.

You see, when we start our mum journey we feel like we have no choice but to put our children first. We worry about being judged. We worry about doing the right thing. We worry about being compared.

The truth is, none of that matters. We are all on our own journey and being a mum doesn't mean you have to lose yourself, who you are and what you want.

Let's look at it a different way. During the air steward's flight safety demonstration, they always say put your oxygen mask on first before attempting to help anyone else.

And why is this?

If you can't breathe then how can you help anyone else?

They don't say, help everyone else first whilst you struggle to breathe!

And that's true in life too. If you're not looking after yourself then eventually you won't be able to look after those you love. And not only that, what example are you setting for others? For the wonderful people in your life who see you as their role model and who you want the best for.

So it's ironic, that when we become a mummy we immediately put ourselves at the bottom of this virtual list. We insist on making sure that everyone else's needs are satisfied first and then wonder why we're too tired or lack time to do anything about ours.

That's why I now help other mums who are feeling the same. Mums who are stuck. Mums who want to make changes. Mums who just need that helping hand to take action. Sometimes you know something is missing but you don't know what it is. I help busy working mums find out what it is and then help them to take action so that they can do something about it.

And that's why I wrote my book, Busy! The working mum's guide to confidently walking life's tightrope.

This book will take you on a journey to discover where the imbalance is in your life and help you determine how you will find the balance that you want, so you can continue balancing throughout your life.

I want to help you easily navigate to a life where you wake up every morning excited by what the day may have in store. Instead of just climbing back onto the treadmill of life and going through the motions.

Just remember, you're doing your best and that is more than good enough.

"Once you're a mom, always a mom. It's like riding a bike, you never forget."

Taraji P. Henson

NICKY MARSHALL

Nicky is an award-winning, international speaker and best-selling author. She is also a mum, nan and wife and loves nothing more than family time.

At 40, Nicky suffered and recovered from a disabling stroke - inspiring a life's mission to make a bigger difference.

Nicky has an accountancy background and twenty years of helping people improve their health and wellbeing under her belt. Combining both, Nicky is a mentor, seasoned workplace facilitator and keynote speaker, inspiring people to discover their own brand of Bounce! Nicky's knowledge, knack for stressbusting, hugs and infectious laugh make her an in demand and popular speaker.

With passion in buckets and a penchant for keeping it simple, Nicky has a unique talent in breaking down the barriers that hold people back from living a life they love.

Be careful if you stand too close - her enthusiasm rubs off!

Follow these links to connect with Nicky:

Website: www.discoveryourbounce.com and www.sleek.bio/nickymarshall

Facebook Group:

www.facebook.com/groups/discoveryourbouncecommunity

Twitter: @dyblifestyle

LinkedIn: www.linkedin.com/in/nickymarshall

Or send her an email: nicky@discoveryourbounce.com

When The Magic Wand Doesn't Work

It was a magical day when I became a mum. I looked down into my newborn's eyes and knew I would fight tigers for this little one. When my second daughter came along, I felt exactly the same.

I'm a polite, mild-mannered soul on most occasions, but very soon I found the voice to speak up for my girls. Always. They were my girls and I was going to protect them.

When Ami had read the entire library in Key Stage One and was refused access to Key Stage Two books, I spoke up. When Kassi faced bullies – pupils and teachers – I spoke up. When I became a single parent, through all of the trauma and despite my voice trembling, I spoke up for my girls.

What I couldn't do was fix everything.

I couldn't fix their broken home.

I couldn't make the bullies go away.

I couldn't always be there when they were scared.

I couldn't stop those chronic health conditions.

I couldn't shield them from heartache.

Even now, as adults, I can't fix, stop, take away or solve their challenges. And it sucks.

I'm sure I'm not the only parent who wishes they could magic away the pain for their babies (because, of course, they will always be my babies!). I actually do have a very nice crystal wand, but try as I might there are some things it just doesn't work on.

As a mum, I know I would suffer any kind of pain myself rather than watch my child go through it.

I've always been a positive person and have lived my life in a way that many would have ruled out as impossible. I have suffered and recovered from a life-changing stroke and stuck two fingers up at the prognosis I was given. In any situation, I always look for potentials, possibilities, opportunities, workarounds… I probably drive those closest to me to frustration as I look for every alternative.

But I have learned that sometimes I need to admit defeat.

There are some things that just truly suck. When someone is unkind. When we hear of someone's actions that just beggar belief. When the daily health struggles that both my girls endure just feel too much for them.

It is at this point that I sometimes have a bit of a cry. Or I swear – a lot. I do my stomping and sulking in front of them, although sometimes I have to carry it on once I'm on my own as it doesn't help them. I run scenarios in my head of what I'm going to do, what I'm going to say to the people that have hurt them. Eventually, as always, I conclude that my energy will be better spent on helping them. This is far better than getting into negative conversations with people that will never change, or lamenting situations that I can't undo.

I sit with them. I hug them. I tell them that it sucks but we're in this together.

In their lives, both have overcome so much. They have made the absolute best of every situation, battled through when most people would have given up. They honestly inspire me so much and I have become a better parent by learning from them.

I know that their situations have given them something else: resilience.

Imagine if I had glossed over all their difficulties, shielded them from challenging situations, distracted them from the issues that needed dealing with, or tried to give them shiny objects so they put off dealing with their grief. They would not be the people they are now. Of course, there were days out, holidays and times when we forgot everything going on and laughed until we cried. I have so many amazing memories of our time together and I treasure every precious moment.

With lots of support, love, discussions, and trial and error they found their own solutions. They found out what they needed to know. They overcame the bullying and abuse, through learning techniques, getting help and being strong. They found ways to adapt and live with their health challenges. They found circles of people to support them. I am so proud of them both.

But it's a balance, isn't it? This parenting lark that we are all supposed to just take to like a duck to water. In the early days, we need to do everything for our children. Every waking hour (even when we wish we could be sleeping!) is spent feeding, clothing, fretting, marvelling… we are their world.

As they grow, we encourage independence and then far too soon they are off to school. Suddenly, they have a new sphere of influence: friends, teachers, books… and their opinions are no longer based on ours alone. Then we have a new balance to tackle – when do we do things for them and when do we stand back?

Now, as a grandparent, I can view all of this with a different perspective. I quake when one of my grandchildren is balancing precariously or leaping around… I see so much more fear than I used to! I remember telling my mum to calm down and stop fretting – I think I'm far worse!

I marvel when they are independently putting on a sock or completing a puzzle… while itching to jump in and do it for them!

I have learned that children are capable of far more than perhaps I allowed my own to do. And that sometimes when they are tired or it's been a busy day, they just want you to do it for them so they can quickly get to bed.

I think it's the same when they become adults.

I remember listening to the opinions of my parents and grandparents growing up. When I got my first job, bought my first car, found my first house, I would turn to my elders for advice and ideas. I didn't always follow it of course, but without it I'm sure I would have made lots more mistakes.

Then the internet arrived.

Now before I'm asked a question, I know my kids will have trawled Google, perhaps asked friends on social media. They will be armed with knowledge that never existed in my day.

Sometimes though, they still want my reassurance, a chat (I would say over a nice cup of tea but neither of them drink it!), or for me to just listen as they work through what's in their head. I love that they can come to me and that I can still be part of that process.

It's tempting to want to do everything for them, even now. My natural problem-solving instincts and 'glass full' nature are still on hand if required. I'm also now quite good at realising that, as much as I want to, I cannot walk their path. I can't solve their problems. I can't see what the future holds. I still wish for that magic wand solution to appear out of thin air and make everything better. Mostly though I choose to love them, support them and be part of their journey through the challenges and the good times – and that's fine with me.

"I came to parenting the way most of us do — knowing nothing and trying to learn everything."

Mayim Bialik

QUENTIN CROWE

Quentin Crowe is an award-winning marketer, business coach, and educator.

He is the Co-founder of QU Co, a community of entrepreneurs who do not identify with traditional 'pale, male and stale' business establishment.

QU Co's mission is to help all entrepreneurs suffering from self-doubt to unleash their hidden potential.

Quentin uses his 'Power of PEERS' methodology to underpin his coaching, mastermind groups and training activities.

Over the last twenty years Quentin has trained more than 5,000 marketers around the world including more unusual locations such as Albania, Bulgaria, Nigeria and Vietnam.

Connect with Quentin:

Website: www.QUco.uk

LinkedIn: www.linkedin.com/in/quentin-crowe-a725345/

Twitter: @QtheMarketer

A Stepfather's Story: How a Lurcher Helped Me Be a Better Parent

I am sitting outside a café enjoying a coffee on a warm July morning. Opposite me sits an eleven-year-old girl. She is the daughter of the woman I have fallen in love with. I am nervous. Not used to communicating with children of this or any age, I struggle to find any line of conversation that interests her. She does not want to engage despite my feeble attempt to win her over with hot chocolate and marshmallow chunks.

Understandably she is icy cold towards me.

Her mother and I have just made a decision that will change her life. We decided to leave our respective spouses and start a new life together.

I'm sure it is hard enough being an eleven-year-old girl in normal circumstances. Having recently moved to senior school you are at the bottom of the pecking order. You also feel increasingly self-conscious and vulnerable as the teenage years approach. To compound matters you have been moved out of the familiar haven of your family home and this unwanted stranger is now part of your life. The adult world has let you down and apart from being stroppy there is nothing you can do about it.

Quite understandably she 'hated me'.

We found a rental property within a few miles of the family home which allowed the children to continue their schooling. We began to settle into some routines and play games together. I had played sport all my life so, for the five-year-old boy, I adopted a very simple approach: throw a ball, kick a ball or hit a ball. Thinking about it, this approach works for boys with any interest in sport regardless of age.

That strategy didn't work at all with this non-sporty 11-year-old girl though. Luckily the children introduced me to a game I have never played before – Jenga. They beat me – repeatedly. Family folklore has it that I kept them playing until well past their bedtimes when I eventually won. We were learning to laugh together, usually at my expense, and the frostiness in the relationship began to thaw.

But this new life was unsustainable as both the children's mother and I were commuting more than three hours a day. After nearly 9 months of this gruelling and unsustainable regime, something had to change. We decided to move closer to my work and family.

This decision would be hugely disruptive for both children. They faced the daunting prospect of leaving behind their familiar surroundings to form a new life. The trust that was so hard-earned eroded.

It took a little time, but both children settled into new schools and started to build new friendships. We established new routines and enjoyed some memorable holidays. At Disneyland Paris I experienced another first in my life – a rollercoaster. Both children took great delight at my abject terror when experiencing that first rollercoaster ride. You may be reading this wondering what sort of life I'd had up to this point, without the joys of Jenga and Rollercoasters, but these shared experiences were forging both trust and our family history.

The Outskirts of Childhood

Just when we felt we were making some real progress, life hit both children with the cruellest of blows.

Their father died.

His passing would affect all of us in differing ways.

Now thirteen and seven years old respectively, these children were dealing with the most adult of issues – the death of a parent. Even now as I write this in my 50s, both my parents are still alive. I still have no comprehension of this level of grief.

Whilst the relationship between the children and myself had been increasingly joyous, I was still little more than a peripheral figure. Now it was time for me to grow up, to step up and take on the father's role.

I hadn't a clue.

The Guiding Dog

When settling into our new home we acquired a black Labrador puppy, or so we thought. Unfortunately, the puppy's provenance was not quite what we expected. When reddish whiskers started to sprout, along with unusually long limbs, it was all too evident that this 'Labrador' was in fact a lurcher.

Monty the lurcher was a dog that didn't lack for character. He had many traits and, depending on one's perspective, not all of them were positive.

He was extremely protective – for example, he guarded the home with total commitment. He would 'welcome' guests at our home's 5-bar gate appearing to levitate, whilst baring his teeth and barking ferociously. A terrifying prospect for any visiting adults.

By contrast he was wonderfully gentle with all children. Monty just wanted to be part of the gang. And they loved him.

As well as being extraordinarily protective, this occasionally deranged lurcher would demonstrate other crucial skills for a novice parent – bravery, to 'just be there', and patient loyalty.

Bravery

Apart from thunder and fireworks, Monty never showed any signs of fearing anything or anybody. It is said that bravery is not being unafraid, but rather the ability to recognise one's fears and do it anyway.

As a father, even a non-biological one, dealing with a teenage daughter was terrifying. There were no instruction manuals to help me navigate this ever-changing landscape. And just when I thought I had caught up, the rules were changed yet again.

Parties, that for ages 11 and 12 were quite innocent, suddenly became more concerning at 13 and provided ample opportunity for negotiation and embarrassment.

What time is the agreed collection time? That time is never late enough.

What to do if they do not emerge at the agreed time? Should you go in and extricate them? On more than one occasion that is exactly what we did!

Then the realisation that your once 'ugly duckling' is emerging into a beautiful swan. There was a memorable occasion travelling through a French airport, when to our horror we realised that all male eyes were fixated on our blossoming teenager. With my hackles up, I have never felt so Monty-like in my desire to scare them away.

These challenges kept coming. From GCSE and A level subject selection to first boyfriend and first break up. From boyfriends we disliked to those we never met. From learning to drive to then coping with the aftermath of the first crash.

For any parent, coping with these rites of passage episodes is daunting. We are exposing these precious innocent creatures to the reality of the adult world. And as an adult I was frightened by this lack of control. Part of me wanted to micromanage, but I learned that as a parent you must face those fears and be brave enough to allow them to find their own way.

Just Be There

During these teenage years, Monty took on the role as a silent counsellor.

My stepdaughter (the children's mother and I had married) would spend many hours with Monty sharing her teenage angst and he just listened unconditionally.

Of course, as a dog he was pleased simply to receive the attention, but unbeknown to him, he was playing a crucial role. He was just there, waiting ready to offer comforting reassurance as and when it was needed.

I should have taken note of this lurcher wisdom.

Instead, I tried too often to impose my pearls of wisdom.

To paraphrase Mark Twain, *"When I was fourteen, my father was so ignorant I could hardly stand to have the old man around. But when I got to be twenty-one, I was astonished at how much he had learned in seven years"*.

Thinking that a young adult would listen to my hard-earned experiences was foolish in the extreme. So 'whatever you do, don't drink the punch!' was of course interpreted as a direct instruction to drink as much of the punch as possible. I will spare you a graphic description of the after-effects.

Meanwhile, our marriage posed a new challenge, one of identity. As their mother now had a different surname, should we invite her children to adopt my surname by hyphenation? We didn't want them to feel in any way pressurised, so after much agonising, we decided against even asking them.

This decision made for some awkward parent-teacher meetings where both my wife and I would be addressed by her previous married name, causing the attending child considerable embarrassment. We faced yet another dilemma. Should we correct the teacher and create even more embarrassment or let it pass? We always chose the latter option.

Much as we would have loved for my stepdaughter to have gone to university, it was clear that academia was not for her. Instead, the 'school of life' beckoned and aged 19, she announced she was going to Australia – for a year. We listened and despite our fears, supported her decision. For the following months she earned as much money as she could to fund the trip whilst also enjoying a busy social life. Inevitably with maturity and greater independence, the more distanced from us she became.

When the day came for her to fly to Australia, I was once more a peripheral figure in her life. As we said our goodbyes at the airport, I felt my parental role was almost at an end. How wrong could I be!

Be Patient

I had doubts about her ability to survive in Australia for a month let alone a year. She had some money, but not enough to survive on for a year. Whilst she had some skills that would get her rudimentary work, she had no qualifications. With her open round-the-world flight paid for, I fully expected her to be flying home within a month or when money ran out, whichever came first. With pride I can say I underestimated her.

Despite a few wobbles, she learned to survive on her wits. She found work, travelled extensively, and developed a mental fortitude that impressed me deeply. I am never sure we will get to know the full truth of her Australian adventure and perhaps it is best we don't. But she did stay the distance.

A year later we met up with her in San Francisco. It was a very emotional meeting for us all. As we toured California as a reunited family, we got to know each other again. Absence had made our hearts grow much fonder. She was now a mature young woman and Mark Twain's quote on adolescence came true. '*She was astonished at how much I had learned*' whilst she had been away. Her travels had changed her perception of me, and we started to bond, now as mutually respectful adults.

Then completely out of the blue she asked me if I would walk her down the aisle when the day came. I could not have been prouder.

When we returned home, the ever-loyal Monty was thrilled to have us all back but especially his special counselling client.

But reality soon hit back. Having been independent for a whole year, and now almost twenty-one years old, she was back in the family fold and inevitably felt constrained. She was adept at getting work to survive, and had found work locally, but there were no long-term plans. What was she going to do for a career? We sat down for a serious chat.

Perhaps being an adult whose opinion she now valued helped, so I began with a simple question: 'Is that it then?' This direct approach seemed to work, and soon afterwards she used her extraordinary life experiences to talk her way on to a graduate scheme for the largest, most prestigious local employer. Within months she was transferred to the city head office and her career took off. She moved to London and eventually settled down with a boyfriend we all liked.

My role as a stepfather seemed complete. Well not quite.

The Proudest Moment

Some years later the aforementioned boyfriend proposed to her. Thankfully she accepted. Twenty years on from that inauspicious first chat, I find myself walking down the aisle with my stunningly beautiful stepdaughter on my arm and truly it is the proudest moment of my life.

A few hours later, I stand up in front of family and friends to deliver my father of the bride speech, the first story I tell almost inevitably features the long deceased but never forgotten Monty.

Be there, be brave, and be patient.

"Having children just puts the whole world into perspective. Everything else just disappears."

Kate Winslet

SIOBHAN PANDYA

Siobhan Pandya, born and raised in Scotland, now resides in Dallas, Texas with her husband, Rupesh and two amazing sons, Ronan and Keaton.

While she loves to spend time with her precious family and friends, she also finds time to help others through her volunteer work. She is currently a Council Member at ACCA (Association of Chartered Certified Accountants) supporting their mission to lead the accountancy profession by creating opportunity.

She is also a Board Member at First Candle, working to end SIDS and other sleep related infant deaths. Siobhan is always guided by her angel, Cailen.

Connect with Siobhan:
Email: siobhanpandya@gmail.com
LinkedIn: www.linkedin.com/in/siobhan-pandya-fcca-4781857/
Website: www.firstcandle.org/

Why Me? Why Anyone?

Life is full of many difficult decisions. As I sat in our apartment, scrolling through pages of nursery designs, I thought I was making one of those decisions. Little did I know that the most difficult decision of our life was yet to come.

Each doctor's appointment was the same.

"You are doing great, the baby is doing great, everything is on track," the doctor would say.

This is exactly what every first-time mum wants and expects to hear. At our 36 week appointment, which included an ultrasound, the message was no different. In fact, we had started counting down to the baby's arrival in days instead of weeks. We went home and followed the same routine and yet something felt strange that night. I sensed a fluttering sensation in my belly and immediately convinced my husband to take me to the hospital. I knew my body and I knew something was wrong. They quickly admitted me and started monitoring us, but not long after came the news that the baby was in distress and there needed to be an emergency c-section.

The next couple of hours were a whirlwind of emotion, adrenaline and exhaustion. Our baby, Cailen, was rushed to the NICU and I was left to rest. A little while later, the doctor slowly walked into my room. She said that what I had been feeling was Cailen having seizures due to the umbilical cord wrapping around his neck and affecting the blood and oxygen flow to his brain. The chances of that happening were close to one in a million – I was that one.

We asked what life would be like for him and she hesitated, then she said, "He's not going to make it. I am sorry. We have him on a ventilator for now." As she left the room, I looked at my husband Rupesh, shook my head and asked him to double check; they must have the wrong baby, they must have a medicine, they must be wrong, they have to be wrong. They were NOT wrong. As Rupesh and I sat in disbelief, we tried to figure out why this was happening to us. It didn't matter how many times we asked the question; the answer was the same each time – we don't know.

We did know one important thing; he was our baby and we were his parents and NOTHING was going to change that. In that moment, we promised each other that we would be the best parents that we could be to our little man. Everything after that moved rapidly; family and friends were called; tears were shed and plans were made. I had just had a c-section, but was not going to let that get in the way of me holding and loving my baby. There would be time for recovery later. Rupesh and I spent every moment in the NICU telling Cailen how much he was loved, how blessed we were to have him as our son and no matter what, he would always be with us. We even tried to get him to pick his favorite parent!

It was on the third day that we made the most difficult decision of our life: we realized that keeping Cailen on a ventilator was for our benefit, as he was sedated the whole time to avoid further seizures. As Rup and I looked at our baby laying there, we knew we had to do the right thing. We informed the doctors that we wanted to take him off the ventilator. It was now up to Cailen to decide when he would be ready for his angel wings. For the next two days we took pictures, told stories, sang songs and did everything we could to fill him with a lifetime of love. I actually tried teaching him how to spell my name – epic fail!

On day 5, around 9pm, I was holding Cailen when I noticed his vitals changing. I could feel him getting weaker in my arms. As the doctors and nurses rushed to check him, we knew that the time had come to say goodbye. We knew it was going to happen but we were still not ready; just one more hug, one more kiss, one more touch. Then our baby became our angel.

Losing your baby is not something that you ever "get over"; instead you learn to live with the memories. You learn why we are told to think about our wildest dreams but not our wildest fears. You learn that not everyone can provide the support needed. You learn that you have to speak your mind without fear of the consequences. You learn that it is okay to be selfish sometimes. You learn that sometimes there is no answer to WHY.

You learn about YOU.

I have always thought of myself as a strong person; someone that can look at the problem in every situation and find an acceptable solution. During my time in the hospital, I realized that some problems are not meant to be solved; they are just meant to be experienced. My experience with Cailen didn't change who I was, instead it changed who I became as I grew older. When I am in a tough situation, I always look back and compare it to what we went through with Cailen and it makes me appreciate three things:

1. Nothing can be as challenging as that experience (autopsies and cremations are best left for TV shows).
2. I have the inner strength and resilience to deal with anything.
3. I miss my baby so much.

Luckily, we have two more boys, Ronan and Keaton, who provide lots of hugs and kisses to help with number 3! One of the most important lessons that both Rupesh and I learned was that each individual deals with each situation differently. We cried, yelled and stayed silent at different times. But we always made sure that we gave one another the space necessary to process what we were going through. My husband provided support at times when I didn't even know that I needed support and by letting him take my pain for a few moments, or make me laugh, I felt human.

While doing this, we felt that it was necessary to get some help and so turned to a psychologist for support. We appreciated the fresh perspective as we learned about how to listen to one another and how to think about the future at some point. We also explored various ways to relax including reiki (a healing technique using energy), yoga and crystal healing. They all helped in separate ways.

Through the journey, I came to the conclusion that I had to make a choice; the choice between continuing the search for WHY or continuing life with my amazing husband. Deep down, I knew that I would never know why this happened to me, why it happened to us, why it happens to anyone and so I stopped searching for answers (at least in this lifetime!). In my opinion, life starts with an empty toolkit and with each experience, we fill it up with a variety of tools; some forever, some for now.

When I think about our experience and how I can help others, the following 'words of Siobhan wisdom' come to mind:

- Be ready to never know WHY
- Always trust your instinct; it can be the difference between life and death
- When everyone wants you to be quiet, shout the loudest
- Keep an open mind; try new things if you think they will help
- Think about what you are going to add to your toolkit based on your experience
- Accept love and support; it will change your perspective
- Understand that time doesn't heal you; you heal you
- Talk about your experiences with a little humor – it definitely helps others feel more comfortable

- Don't compare your experience to anyone else's – each one is unique
- Be thankful for what you gained; it's more fulfilling than thinking about what you lost
- Don't feel bad about remembering your experience, no matter how much time has passed
- Expect others to move on: this is not their experience
- Similar to airplane life vests, take care of yourself before you try and take care of others
- Chocolate always helps, preferably Cadburys
- It is what it is (this one should be a standard tattoo!)

Both Rupesh and I take comfort from the thought that our angel, Cailen, is watching over us all and that he knows how much he is loved and missed each and every day. We are so fortunate that we can share these experiences together, support one another and watch our boys fill up their life toolkits. Although I will never know why this happened, I know that I will do my best to make sure that it doesn't happen to anyone else, which is why I am a Board Member at First Candle, a not for profit organization working to end Sudden Infant Death Syndrome and other sleep-related infant deaths as well as support families who have had a loss.

But after all these words, the most important point to make is that I would not change any of it. It may sound odd, but I truly believe that everything happens for a reason; I may not know that reason today or any day, but I know that it is a part of our journey, my journey.

This is the life I was given and I need to live it to the best of my ability.

"Being a mama can be tough, but always remember in the eyes of your child, no one does it better than you."

Unknown

SUE TETLEY

Sue lives in Suffolk with her husband, daughter and cat.

Sue works as a Thrive Programme Coach, teaching people the skills and self-insight to overcome mental health issues themselves. She is also a mindset fitness coach helping women to gain confidence to overcome social anxiety and limiting beliefs around exercise.

Sue loves doing triathlons and open water swimming. She is a This Girl Can Ambassador and Mental Health Champion.

Sue aspires to be a great role model for her young daughter who was adopted as a baby and show her that if you work hard and believe in yourself, anything is possible.

Connect with Sue:

Website: www.thriveprogramme.org/sue-tetley

Email: sue.tetley@thriveprogramme.org

Facebook: www.facebook.com/thrivewithsue

Instagram: @thrive.with.sue/

Website: www.suetetleywellness.co.uk

Facebook: www.facebook.com/suetetleywellness

Instagram: @sue.tetleywellness/

Our Adoption Story

As a 25 year old and newly married I had my whole life in front of me. It was exciting with so many possibilities. Having a family was something I'd envisaged for myself at some point, but not for a while. I had just about learnt to look after myself and perhaps a few plants. A pet was a bit of a stretch too far at that point in my life, let alone caring for a baby.

Fast forward 4 years to age 29 and Phil and I started to discuss having a family. We began to think that perhaps we were old enough now to be able to care for another human being.

One Phone Call Can Change Everything

We then spent the next few years trying to get pregnant. The testing process commenced. They started with me, running blood tests to check hormone levels. Then it was Phil's turn.

I still remember the phone going and it being the local GP surgery. They wouldn't speak to me, they wanted to speak to Phil. It was a difficult conversation. They needed another sample as they found no sperm at all. In that one call our whole world changed.

This was the start of the roller-coaster that was infertility treatment.

Like many people we were blissfully ignorant, assuming that if we wanted a child, it would just happen. We spent many years going through IVF treatment. During that time, I found it increasingly difficult to spend time with friends who were pregnant or who had babies and young children.

There were triggers everywhere, especially on social media. Mother's Day was getting unbearable, reminding me of what I yearned for but couldn't have. All over Facebook there were images of children and women posting about how blessed they were and how wonderful their children are.

I wanted to either cry or just be sick at these smug perfect family images.

The Agony of Choice

It was tough knowing when to stop, accepting we could never have our own biological child. We couldn't continue indefinitely, the impact on our lives and mental and physical well-being was getting too much. After 8 years of treatment, we had to take back control of our lives and call an end to the process. It was incredibly painful, but a relief once the decision had been made.

We had a decision to make. Do we just stop and enjoy a life without children, or do we have a family in a different way? The whole process was filled with choice after choice that we would never have had to make if we'd had a child naturally.

I tried to imagine my life without children and knew that it was something I didn't want. When we started the infertility treatment, I never imagined it wouldn't work. During the last few rounds of IVF, the idea of adoption started to become a real possibility. Ultimately, it's not how you have a family, but what you end up with in the end that matters. Our perspective was changing, and we were adapting to this new reality.

Adoption

After a break, we started stage one of the adoption process, consisting of DBS checks, contacting friends and family to check we were suitable candidates. Also checking the house and garden to establish what we would need to do to childproof it. We were assigned a social worker. There were courses to attend, and we had to do some voluntary work with children for a few months. It didn't matter that I was an experienced paediatric nurse!

Some of the requirements were interesting in child proofing our home. We had a stream at the bottom of the garden so clearly needed to put up some sort of fence. We asked the social worker how high she would like this to be. She proceeded to point to the 7ft fence bordering on our neighbour's garden! Unless this child was a champion pole vaulter, this was rather over the top! It would have totally blocked our view of the stream and the beautiful countryside. After some negotiation, she was happy with the end result.

We had heard many stories, from people we knew, about how hard it had been for them to adopt and how they had given up. However, the process had become much quicker, the government putting in legislation to speed up the process.

Having gone through a huge level of uncertainty with IVF, I found adoption much easier and far less stressful. The process of adoption could be seen by many to be rather intrusive. However, after lots of internal ultrasounds, bloods, injections and painful procedures, a conversation with a social worker seemed easy.

I was confident that we would be successful. We had been married for 15 years and both had a stable job. If an experienced paediatric nurse, who was also a mental health professional, couldn't adopt, then who could?

Stage two consisted of a 'home study' where we spent two hours every other week talking to the social worker about aspects of our lives and our own childhoods. The social worker then submitted a report for the adoption panel.

It was then time for the adoption panel. We had been given the questions in advance. Our whole future was in their hands. I didn't think there would be an issue, but you can never be 100% sure. After answering all the questions, we had to go into another room whilst they discussed us. It was an anxious wait that seemed to take forever, even though it was only 10 or 15 minutes. I was a nervous wreck. This decision would change our lives. We were called back into the room. To our enormous relief and delight, we were approved and would soon be a mummy and daddy!

More Decisions to be Made

We had to consider what child we would like. This again was tough, but we had to be brutally honest with ourselves and the social worker. We just wanted a 'normal' family life. Yes, if we discovered issues after adopting a child, then we would deal with it, like you would if you had your own biological child. However, we had to tick what issues/disabilities we would be happy to adopt a child with. This was a huge list and I found it emotionally challenging to do this. However, if we were not honest and couldn't handle a situation, then the adoption could break down and this would be traumatic for the child.

We also had to think whether we wanted a boy or a girl and what age. Also things like what hair and eye colour. It was incredibly detailed, and we felt we were overthinking everything.

We Have a Match!

It was then a waiting game to get a match. It took about 4 months before we got the call. I was in the local gym about to walk out of the doors. I saw a few missed calls and then the phone rang again. It was our social worker. She had a match for us! I was so excited and in a daze trying to take it all in. It was an 8-month-old little girl. This was becoming real. We met up with our social worker and she showed us a few photos. We got a report about her with details on her background. We were happy with the match and started the process. We had to then be approved for the match which didn't take long.

We met the foster carers and their social worker at our house, and they brought along some photos of her. A time scale was then arranged to start the introductions. This was incredibly detailed and the time we spent with her increased each day over an 8-day period. For older children this would take longer. We had to provide some photos of both of us together that would be turned into place mats so she could start eating her dinner off them and getting used to what we looked like. When we came to meet her, we would then seem familiar. We were also asked to do a talking book, recording our voices and have pictures of our house. I decorated this with lots of stickers to make it colourful before I sent it to the foster carers.

The Day We Met Our Child

It was time to meet our daughter for the first time at her foster carers' house. Jessica was now 11 months old and walking. Imagine getting out of your car and knocking on the door of a person you've met once, to meet your child for the first time. Knowing that as soon as that door opens, your life will be changed forever. I had been waiting to be a mummy for so long and now it was about to happen. It's a surreal and amazing experience. I was trying to keep my emotions under wraps as I had no idea how I would react. When we finally saw our little girl, all of the years and years of physical and emotional pain suddenly drifted away in that moment of seeing her for the first time.

Getting to Know Our Daughter

We seemed to bond with Jessica straight away. She accepted us and she was a happy baby. We had to rapidly get to know her and meet her needs. Phil had taken 3 months' adoption leave and I had taken a year off my nursing job, so we both muddled through together. We just threw ourselves into the deep end and took her out. We had no idea how she would react in certain situations, but just had to go with it.

I remember only having her a few days before taking her to Tot Rock in the local library. I still felt at that time like I was 'pretending' to be her mum and would soon wake up from a dream.

She settled in well and we just kept to the same routine as the foster carers. We only had her a few days before her first birthday. We had a little party inviting over a few friends. I also went into town and bought her lots of new clothes and toys. I found this emotional. She had come to us with literally two bags. That was it. Her whole life in these two shopping bags. Although this was extremely sad, I went about rectifying this. Even now, I get emotional thinking about it.

This little girl was going to have a great life and we would be there to support her in anything she wanted to do. We knew the background of her birth mother which was extremely sad too. The moment we adopted her, we had transformed her future and made anything possible for her. She has the chance to be whatever she wants to be in life. This is the gift of adoption: the unconditional love and support that transforms a child's destiny in one decision.

Once Jessica had been with us for 6 months, we were legally allowed to adopt her. This was a fantastic day. We went to the local family court for a celebratory ceremony. We became her official parents, and her birth certificate was changed.

Life Now

Four years on, I cannot imagine life without her. Yes, it was a huge lifestyle change for us, but one that we yearned for. Our house has been totally transformed; ornaments replaced by toys!

Jessica knows she was adopted, and we keep in contact with her foster carers. We will gradually tell her more as she gets older. It's so important to be open about the adoption rather than her finding out as a teenager. The implications to her mental health and her relationship with us would be significant and her trust in us would be gone.

I would encourage anyone to adopt. There are so many children out there desperately in need of a loving home. It would be impossible to love Jessica any more than we do, genetics don't come into it. She is our little girl. She is truly flourishing and is such a happy active child we can ask for no more.

"Anyone who ever wondered how much they could love a child who did not spring from their own loins, know this: it is the same. The feeling of love is so profound, it's incredible and surprising." — Nia Vardalos

"A mother's arms are more comforting than anyone else's."

Princess Diana

VICKY JIMENEZ

Vicky's background is in ICT, she holds a degree in Computing and is a qualified secondary school teacher. She is trained in understanding Autism, peer mentoring, suicide prevention and is a Mental Health First Aider. She loves spending time with her family and dog and making people laugh!

Vicky has lived experience of mental health difficulties. She is passionate about using her experiences of trauma and recovery to impart hope and empower others to live their best life. Her mantra is "you are loved exactly as you are and you are enough!" During the COVID-19 lockdowns she has found much joy in reaching many who are isolated, bringing them connection with others who feel the same and equipping them with tools to help ride the storms of their darkest days.

As a mum to one grown up son, she hopes that our next generation can learn to see that they are enough exactly as they are. Regardless of background, everyone has gifts that they can bring to this world and with the right support and self-belief anything is possible!

Connect with Vicky:

Email: getvickyj@hotmail.com

Facebook: www.facebook.com/vicky.jimenez.9480/

Instagram: @vicky.jimenez.official/

The Gift of Good Memories

One of the greatest gifts you can give a child is good memories. I don't have many of those but that's another story. It has been my main motivation in parenting. I wanted things to be different to my own childhood.

My son wasn't planned. He was conceived with love, but out of wedlock and in an environment of disgrace and guilt. For the shame I had brought on my family, and ultimately God, because of the strict religious upbringing I'd had. I'm not describing the 50s here, it was 1990 and I was 17, terrified of my violent father, eager to get out of my homelife and desperate to be loved. The man I'd fallen in love with was a tall, dark Spaniard that I would have done anything for.

My mum told me I could stay at home, she would help me bring my child up and I didn't have to get married. My father threatened to kick me out and docked his contribution to household finances, telling me if I was adult enough to get pregnant, I could pay my own contribution to the household bills now. As you can imagine, it wasn't an environment that I wanted to bring my son up in. Begrudgingly my parents gave their permission for me to marry at 17 years old. Six months later my beautiful baby boy was born, two weeks early, after a lengthy 20-hour labour. The midwife who had cared for me the day I started my labour returned to do her shift the next day, expecting me to be a new mum, and actually went on to deliver my baby!

We lived in a maisonette, it was down some steps below the level of the road. The second bedroom backed onto the foundation of the road and it was so damp the plaster was falling off the wall. I couldn't let my son sleep in there so he slept next to me in our bedroom.

Without going into too much detail about the breakdown of my marriage, let's just say it didn't last and I soon realised that I was bringing this baby up on my own. My husband had minimal involvement in his life.

A few days after I came home from hospital my son stopped breathing and turned blue, I was terrified. I thought he was going to die but then he caught his breath again. Arrangements were made to take him into the John Parkes children's unit and that's where I stayed for a couple of weeks. I slept on a camp bed next to my son in his cot, who by now had a tube up his nose and a sensor which could tell if he stopped breathing. It seemed the damp in our home had contributed to the problem and he had to stay in until his chest cleared. In addition, my milk was drying up with all the stress and he wasn't putting on enough weight, so I sat there for hours with a breast pump determined that I was going to feed my own child. Ultimately, I had to admit defeat and I felt broken; I'd brought all this shame on my family and now I felt I was a total failure as a mum.

I was determined to get out of that flat. There was a new development of social housing being built at the top of the hill and I tirelessly fought to get our names down for one. Thankfully this was successful and just after my son was a year old, we moved into a brand new two-bedroom semi-detached house. It was like winning the lottery!

Unfortunately, as time passed my son saw things that he shouldn't have seen. I regret that I didn't get out earlier, but I'm grateful that I did get out in the end. It wasn't easy, as I still loved my husband. It had been indoctrinated into me that marriage was for life, and that's how I genuinely felt, but it wasn't to be. Nor was it a healthy environment to bring a child up in. So, after several times that my husband had left me and then returned, I asked him to go for good and started my journey as a single parent.

It was clear early on that my son was very clever. I did lots of educational games with him at home and he could read before he started school. He always got good reports, his smile was gorgeous, he had his dad's olive skin and teachers said he was a pleasure to have in the class, but he would have total meltdowns that I couldn't understand.

I faced a lot of criticism, 'you're too soft', 'you do too much for him', 'if he was mine, I'd give him a good hiding', 'he doesn't behave like that with me, he knows he can't get away with it', 'why is he doing that?', 'why is he making that noise?', 'can't he stand still for one minute?' and on and on it went. I often doubted myself, but I carried on doing things my way regardless.

It was towards the end of primary school that my son started to have problems. I couldn't get him into school, we were always late and sometimes he would be screaming not to make him go in. I was having to drive around the corner, right to the school door, as I couldn't get him to walk the short distance. It was incredibly sad to see him like that. I discovered he was self-harming; he was feeling suicidal and eventually he was referred to a psychiatrist and diagnosed with Major Depressive Disorder. He was nine, he had given up on life and it was heart-breaking. The regular trips to the child guidance unit at the hospital started and continued for some years.

Like any child, his move to secondary school was an anxious time. It's a huge change going to big school, being the youngest, making new friends and adjusting to lots of different teachers. I needn't have worried because his first report was absolutely glowing, filled with comments of how well he was doing and what a pleasure he was to teach. To top it off he had been placed on the gifted and talented register. He went on an enrichment weekend with other talented youngsters, which went well. I couldn't have been more proud; I remember I was buzzing when we got home. I was filled with hope that maybe this was the challenge he needed and things would improve, and they did for a while.

One thing that I'm grateful to my mum for was telling us that, "There's no such word as can't!" I've lived by that and brought my son up by it, except with the addendum, 'if you have the right support'. Shortly after my marriage broke up for the final time, I started college as a mature student. I was too afraid to sign up for the course initially and I remember going to the first lesson and feeling completely overwhelmed by the subject of computer programming, but afterwards I still went to the office and signed up! I did an Access course which led to an Higher National Diploma, a degree and finally a Postgraduate Certificate in Education. Each time I began by saying, 'I don't think I'll be able to do that', but doing it anyway and eventually qualifying as a specialist ICT Secondary School Teacher.

One day whilst doing my degree, I was on the park and ride bus going from university back to my car, when I had a call from my son. He was upset that his art teacher hadn't been very nice, he wasn't very clear about what she had said and I suggested that maybe it wasn't about him. Perhaps she was stressed, had an argument with her husband or something, and he'd just borne the brunt of it. We agreed that we'd see how it went and I didn't hear any more until a couple of months later when one of his friends came for tea. It was a feeling of total shock and anger when his friend began to tell me the events of that lesson. The reports had just been published and my son had scored unusually low in that subject, which baffled me as it was so out of character. His friend described how shocked the whole class had been at the way this teacher had spoken to my son. I wrote everything down as he was saying it, so as not to get it wrong. My son hadn't told me the whole story because he couldn't work out if she had actually said these things, or if he'd imagined it. Clearly he hadn't and further investigation by the school revealed that all of the class had been really shocked that day and concerned for my son. Many random children that were interviewed reiterated the same account of what had happened.

After that he never really returned to school regularly and the psychiatrist recommended he be home schooled as he wasn't coping with mainstream school, so he was enrolled into an online academy. I had just qualified as a secondary school teacher, something I'd worked so hard as a single parent to achieve. There was no question about it; I had to put my career on hold to help my son get through his education. An adult had to be home with him for tutors to come in and I knew he would struggle to be motivated to get onto his online lessons without me cajoling him into it. So I created a timetable for each week and planned a routine for his home education and I never went back to teaching as a career.

He didn't get as many teaching hours as he would in mainstream school, but he did well and managed to get the grades he needed to be accepted into college for A Levels. Towards the end of college, I discovered by accident that he had previously been diagnosed with Autistic Spectrum Disorder when he was younger. I was shocked; how could I go to all the appointments at the hospital and no one told me?! Had I known earlier, there would have been more support available, but in spite of this he'd got into college. It was a real struggle, but he persisted and completed his courses. Eventually, after a number of unconditional offers, he got a place at the university he wanted to go to.

When there were problems, I encouraged him to jump through whatever hoops there were to get where he wanted to be and try to ignore those people who would drag him down. I'd tell him they wouldn't even be in his life the following year and to keep his focus on where he wanted to be and not let them take that away. I was immensely proud to see and attend his many achievements: his gold Duke of Edinburgh award at St

James Palace, Medical School Summer Camp Presentation, Young Person of the Year Award, Degree Graduation, Mountain Leader and many other awards and special events.

I had been out most nights doing Mum's Taxi for various clubs; Air Cadets, Warhammer club, ice hockey, figure skating, ice disco, and young volunteer's group. When opportunities came up for travel, I encouraged him to go and often had to sell things to find the money. He's been to far more places than I could dream of and they have been wonderful life experiences for him, giving him a broader outlook on life and other cultures.

As a parent, all I knew was that I wanted his experience of childhood to be different to mine. I didn't want my son to grow up and ask, 'why did you let that happen to me?', 'you were the adult, why didn't you leave?', 'why didn't you protect me?' I wanted him to have every opportunity that I could possibly give him and I would give up everything to do the same again. At the end of the day, he was my child and I was the one that had to live with how I did things, not any of these doubters or naysayers. Just me, his mum, doing her best for him.

There's a saying, 'the proof is in the pudding'. It's funny because no one is criticising me anymore for the way I brought my son up. He's got a degree and is finishing his Masters. He has a responsible job, makes a difference in his community, has a home and has recently married. He's battled through put downs and sometimes blatant discrimination, whilst at university and also at work. He's managed the struggles that have come with Autism, but also has harnessed the amazing superpowers it gives him too. He's faced mental health struggles and found ways of managing those dark times.

I'm unashamedly proud of the man he has grown up to be. Often single parents are not portrayed well in the media, but I muddled through the challenges in the best way I knew how and did things my way. He remembers the things we did together, he knows I always had his back, whatever the problem and he often tells me how proud he is of me. Most importantly, I am proud because he is happy. He values the meaningful things in life, which are often not monetary but connection, being out in nature, mental wellbeing and having compassion for others. He knows he is enough and loved exactly as he is.

When he talks about childhood memories, it's never about how much I bought him, it's about the things we did together, the battles we got through, the positive way I spoke to him and the way I made him feel. My hope is that the legacy I'm leaving will be remembered long after I'm gone and something he will apply to his own parenting. It wasn't perfect, I don't know all the answers, but I do know that toxic relationships and behaviour do not nourish a child. Whether you're a couple or a single parent, if you had these growing up, put them behind you and resolve to be the start of a new way for your own family.

Children don't come with manuals and troubleshooting guides, but you have the power to change their destiny and mould their future. Teach them that they are enough exactly as they are. They might not be academic, but they all bring something valuable to this world. Don't be swayed by other people. You know your child best and you have to live with the way you parented them and the long-term effects of that on their life. I truly believe if you try to create good memories, those feelings of love will be with them for life, giving them resilience to face the ups and downs, and that's a priceless gift worth having!

"Motherhood is the greatest thing and the hardest thing."

Ricki Lake

EXPERT TIPS

EMILY JOLLIFFE

Emily is a couples and 1-1 counsellor, specialising in supporting parents through tough times.

She offers tailored wellbeing/autism coaching and small group programmes on themes like setting boundaries with love and working with children's motivations. Emily offers Zoom sessions to clients in the UK and internationally. She loves walk and talk sessions with those in the Bath/Frome area.

Emily is a certified counsellor in the Option Process Dialogue and an accredited coach with the Independent Authority for Professional Coaching and Mentoring.

Before she retrained as a counsellor and coach, Emily worked in education and conflict resolution.

Connect with Emily:

Website: www.getclarity-letgo.co.uk/

Facebook group for parents of autistic children:

www.facebook.com/groups/specialparentingtogether

Book a call:

hello.dubsado.com:443/public/schedulerGroup/62066a700e964930cc0bf0
8c

Instagram: @emilycounsellorautismcoach/

LinkedIn: www.linkedin.com/in/emily-jolliffe-331b36a

Our Own Attitude and Actions Help Our Autistic Children Grow

Our attitude was essential in how we helped our autistic son. This attitude is based on love and acceptance and believing our children teach us at least as much as we might teach them!

The techniques I teach and coach parents of children with extra needs, stem from this attitude and belief. The first four are adapted from the things I learned in my Son Rise Programme® training, which helped our son manage in mainstream school and make friends. The last two I add from my own experience:

- Balancing hope and acceptance for your child
- Carving out one to one time to follow your child's motivations and join their repetitive, self-soothing isms or stims
- Celebrations are to social as sun is to sunflowers
- Managing meltdowns and setting boundaries with love
- Helping our children with friendships
- Filling your own cup first

Balancing Hope and Acceptance for Your Child

Your hopes for your autistic child are important. Some of us have been told what they won't achieve. A Harley Street occupational therapist came to our then 7-year-old's school and told me my son would never develop 'theory of mind': the knowledge that other people have thoughts and perspectives that are different from ours. Coming away from that meeting, I thought: "but he loves pranks!" Pranks depend on the person being pranked not knowing they'll be pranked.

He'd already proved them wrong. Other teachers thought he might get involved in violent crime. What if we'd been swayed by these dramatic projections for his future and replaced love and acceptance with fear?

Your hopes for your child might be that they become independent, potty trained, a good sleeper, happy, have friends, work, try new things, express themselves, share hobbies and more. Each day, we can take small steps together towards achieving these hopes and goals. Along the way, we can celebrate our child's beautiful eye contact, sharing, tasting new food, touching gently or working out a conflict instead of taking it out on someone.

What we hope for, we will model and work towards. We can be optimistic and put no limits on what our child can achieve. They're their own person!

As their parents we love our kids the most, want the most for them and can spend the most time with them. Professionals may have useful inputs for sure, but they're not changing our children's beds in the middle of the night. We put the time in: we get to have hopes too!

It's a balance of accepting our kids, just as they are in this moment, **and** having hopes for them. Not **needing** to change a hair on their head, **but** inviting them to stretch. Loving them as they are today **and** waving the flag of social interaction by being fun and useful to them. I don't claim to have that balance right every day, sometimes I've put myself and my son under too much time pressure - and it usually backfires! We're not in control of our child or any other person. To let go of the illusion of control can feel liberating.

We can hope for the things our child is already on track to achieving, and for those that seem a way off yet. Both hopes will inform our goals; hope moves us closer, one step at a time, day by day. Allow yourself to hope for your family: no one's allowed to extinguish that.

One to One Time

Carving out one to one focused time with our child (special time/play time), actively demonstrates our love to our child. What we love, we prioritise and give time to. We started by giving our son 15 minutes dedicated one to one time most days, in his bedroom with the door shut. He received 30 minutes – 15 from each parent. We followed his motivations: we would read his favourite books and magazines, sing, play instruments and games, write stories, draw, knit, throw and catch, roll around, massage, or talk and listen about fishing, aeroplanes, bushcraft, and birds of prey. All were directed from him and his passions. Several times we tied red wool criss-crossing his whole bedroom to simulate laser beams we could climb through but not touch!

If you do one to one time daily: wonderful. Do what is possible in your life. You might enjoy it so much you rearrange your life so you can do more! Do it because you want to and at a time you won't be distracted or interrupted. That means no phones or electronics! Revel in the chance to be childlike again, knowing it's deeply bonding and healing for you both. This strong bond lays the ground for everything you hope for with your child's future relationships. Spending time in their world is enriching for them and us.

Joining Isms

In one to one time, when your child is exclusive and isming (stimming), for example doing a repetitive, exclusive action which seems to soothe them, simply join them in that. If they hum, hum. If they pace, pace. If they jump, jump. Follow their lead with genuine curiosity to see what they might be getting out of the activity. Joining is a way to show we unconditionally accept and love our child as they are. It's deeply bonding.

Celebrations Are to Social as Sun is to Sunflowers

Celebrating our child gives **us** a clear way to encourage what we want them to do more of. It feels great too! **They** gain a clear understanding of what is helpful to them, which makes the world less unpredictable. Sometimes we need to redirect our child, explain how their action affects someone else, or set a loving boundary. We want to make sure we have a kind, loving balance in our interactions with them, so it's important to notice all the celebratable things they're doing too.

'Catch them being good' was the byword of our son's second school: a positive approach. I would replace 'good' with 'social', for autistic children: some social actions and interactions might well be more work than for a neurotypical child. We can show them our delight by celebrating and being visibly grateful they're making that effort with us. We're mostly not raised in celebratory cultures so it is important to practice this new habit. Have fun with it!

With the volunteers we trained to play with our son, I noticed the more they celebrated **themselves**, the easier they found it to celebrate **him**. When our child knows we love them, they stretch to do new things, they follow the celebration as a sunflower turns to the sun. Quite simply, they will likely do that new thing more. This facilitates our child's brain to form new neural pathways that help them and our relationship.

Perhaps your child could talk for 9 hours a day about railway trains or possums or Pokémon. Celebrations help us focus on, "I love you and want you to share your fascination with **me**!" You don't have to spend 9 hours listening. Just listen in your one to one time. Be enthusiastic with your child each time they do something you love and want to see more of, and they'll know to do more of it.

Managing Meltdowns

The question I'm most often asked by parents is how do I manage in the moments when things are really hard, maybe furniture flying or someone getting hurt?

First, know that your child is doing the best they can in that moment, they may be overstimulated, and your own sense of ease is the most helpful thing you can bring.

But how **do** you calm yourself when no one around you is remotely calm? By knowing that it makes a difference to the situation. We know our own response, even our tone of voice, can contribute to our child's well-being in fraught moments. We can all think of occasions when we were more or less effective at dealing with our child's meltdown.

Here are some beliefs, feelings and actions that help me be more useful during and beyond the meltdown moments:

Beliefs – which fuel our feelings and actions:
- "My child's outburst means nothing about me."
- "They're getting something out of their system."
- "I am in charge of my own reaction."
- "They want to tell me something."

Feelings – can be set as intentions:
- "I want to feel…"
Peaceful, connected, at ease, playful, loving, curious.

Actions

Start by making yourself safe and others if need be.

Be present, breathe, count your breaths, walk away, observe, soften your shoulders and jaw, listen, and be selective and concise with your words.

You don't **have** to do any of these things; knowing they're even possible 'in the heat of the moment' could make a difference and might be a sharp contrast from our own upbringing. A single option above could make the situation feel less 'hot' and have a positive ripple effect.

How we show up matters. We, the adults, have a choice. Remembering that choice in the moments where our kids may be struggling to self-regulate is the first step.

As I started my journey of parenting my autistic son, trialing different ways, I spent months berating myself if I made the 'wrong' choice. Like thinking if my son swore, or if I raised my voice it meant I was a 'bad mum'. Feel free to skip that step and save yourself a tonne of discomfort! Just like our children, we're doing the best we can with what we know. We're able to learn more when our mind and hearts are open to learning, and we're present in the moment. When we judge ourselves, we can't be present or open.

Setting Boundaries with Love

In Russell Brand's interview with Brené Brown, he asks her how long you have to set a boundary with your child for it to stick. She replies:

"The question to ask is, how many times do you back slide? It only takes one time for your child to know you are full of shit."

Brené Brown adds that our children learn their boundaries from experiencing ours. If it matters to you that they can keep themselves safe as teens and adults, modelling clear loving boundaries from a young age is crucial. If we model giving in when they whine, it may be harder for them to find their voice and conviction in their own times of challenge.

Clear consistent boundaries help our children feel safe and held. Autistic children often have high control needs as the world may seem unpredictable, so clarity and consistency from us will help. We may not have experienced this as children; much of this parenting approach departs radically from previous generations. Cause and effect is a large part of how humans learn. Safe boundaries involve **consequences and consistency**.

Parenting Protocols by Barry, Samahria and Bryn Kaufman describes three levels of consequences:

1. Natural consequences: fire burns skin or the dog won't trust you if you hurt her. The universe provides these without us needing to teach.

2. Logical consequences: these work in the parent's favour and also take account of the age and stage of the child. E.g. 'Let's tidy up the rice you threw on the floor together'.

3. Parent imposed consequences: to be used most sparingly! The ones you make up on the fly and need to not backslide on. They have no natural law or even the logic of cause and effect. Children question these most as they often make no sense to them.

There's no pressure to decide on a consequence in the heat of the moment. We can give ourselves powerful thinking time. It's worth considering which boundaries are key to us and drop some of the battles.

Helping our Children with Friendships

"We are our child's first friend" is the most useful thing I learnt about encouraging friendships. Our children learn relationships from us, so let's be kind, helpful ambassadors of social interaction so they can practice predictably. This stage took us some years.

Friendship and interaction look different to different people, even more so when you add in neuro differences. Neurodiverse and neurotypical friendships can look different. It's important to hold that in mind and not impose our standards or beliefs about friends on our children. They may have different needs and wants, including around their number of close friendships. Not everyone has a best friend or a group of friends who all know each other. Some enjoy groups, others thrive on one to one time or more solo time.

We might contact our friends by text or spend hours talking. We might share activities and common interests. Online friendships are now possible. Chitchat and knowing each other's background may be less important to autistic people. It's worth remembering that most children chat and engage differently from adults. Often they throw themselves into their activity with no preamble.

There are many ways we can help our child make friends and sustain those friendships. When your child is ready to have successful short play dates one to one, notice if they mention someone, invite that neighbour, classmate or friend over for a short, focused time when you are on hand and can observe initially. We want to set them up for success, so end it when it's going well.

As they get older, we can encourage them to meet friends outside of the home, for a drink, film, walk, shop. As always, they'll do this when they're ready and want it enough, so no pressure if they're not there yet. Conversely, if they want more independence than you feel they're ready for, walk them through the stages to get there.

Encourage group activities and hobbies. These can sometimes be before a one to one friendship if your child is motivated. Our son enjoyed martial arts classes for several years: it was a very controlled environment with clear instructions that helped him be successful. He was praised for his listening skills and was eager to do well. Just as in one to one time, follow their motivation, be it drama or dance, cubs or climbing.

Make hangouts short and with a purpose, e.g. 30-60 minutes at the park or going to a river to paddle for younger ones, or cinema, bushcraft, basketball or bowling for teens and tweens. Sharing an activity together removes pressure to chat. We also want to help our child identify and resolve issues or disagreements, perhaps moving on if a friend is unkind. Encourage them to reflect back on relationships, and how other people might perceive a situation.

Fill Your Own Cup First

The cornerstone of parenting is looking after ourselves to keep fuel in our tank. Parenting an autistic child can feel all-consuming at times, but it doesn't define us. If you grew up with the model of self-sacrificial parenting, looking after yourself will feel new. As Penny Wincer, author of Tender: The Imperfect Art of Caring, says:

"When you put yourself last all the time, in the end, everyone else suffers."

I know others suffer if I respond to my distressed child when I'm super tired and overwhelmed. I'm very likely to snap. We can't employ the autism connection techniques I've outlined, when we're crying into our coffee with exasperation and fatigue.

I firmly believe that when we focus on our needs first, through learning, being present and releasing stress, we become more available and useful to our children.

I deal with the challenges of family life and being mum to our neurodivergent sons much more effectively when I prioritise my sleep, and nurture myself with what I enjoy.

Put your own oxygen mask on first. Help yourself first **in order** to help those you love. Here's my recommendation for when you feel overwhelmed or out of balance: write down or create a mind map of what fills your cup. That might be chatting with friends, going for a walk, reading a poem or a novel, exercising, making things, having a bath, cooking, cuddling your pet, laughing at comedy, an evening in or out with a friend or partner. Include free, cheap things and some you can do with children.

Once you've listed them, work out when and how often you can do things that make your heart sing, and the practicalities like timing and childcare if necessary. Let's not make self-care another stick to beat ourselves with! Simply notice what in your life you aren't enjoying and see if you can switch that for something that fills your cup. Being rested and energised will elevate your efforts to support your child in these ways. Restorative rest, connection and self expression are so vital to your health and wellbeing. These are important in their own rights.

I trust this is helpful to you. I support individual parents, couples and teenagers, as well as small workshops looking at these areas in more depth. Contact me if that sounds useful.

"Having children obviously changes your priorities, but when you start to see life through these innocent eyes and seeing everything for the first time, you appreciate the small things."

Nick Cannon

HELEN FARMER INTERVIEWS REBECCA SCOTT

Rebecca Scott, Employability and Opportunities Manager at the University of Bristol, has been awarded an MBE for her work in supporting disadvantaged communities in Bristol.

For more than 15 years Rebecca has worked with individuals and their families to support them in accessing a range of education and employment opportunities with a particular focus on the many disparities in the areas of disability and race.

Combining her own personal experiences with her professional knowledge, Rebecca has held multiple voluntary positions across the city in organisations such as Autism Independence and Changing Your Mindset that provide support to those experiencing barriers in accessing education and employment, through the sharing of knowledge, connecting of existing services and the developing of new ones.

In recent years Rebecca has launched eXcel Bristol and JOIN US!, the University of Bristol's apprenticeship expansion project which aspires to provide a blend of employment and education opportunities in the form of an apprenticeship to those who may not have traditionally considered the University as an employer and encountered barriers entering employment.

Website: www.bristol.ac.uk/inclusion/diversify-your-workforce/

Autism Independence CIC: www.facebook.com/AutismIndependence/

Changing Your Mindset: www.facebook.com/changingyourmindsetevolve

New Year's Honours for Rebecca Scott:

www.bristol.ac.uk/news/2021/december/rebecca-scott-mbe.html

Autism, Assumptions and Life as a Single Mum.

Diversity & Inclusion expert Helen Farmer met with Rebecca Scott to talk about her parenting experience. This is their conversation.

Let's start with your experience, this is all about your story. In your own words, can you tell us about your experience of being a parent?
So, it's going to be short and sweet for this one. It has been very, very challenging and also quite an isolating experience. I'm a single mum with one child, a 17-year-old boy. He is an ethnic minority, so a black boy. He suffers from autism, and higher anxiety, that is high functioning autism, and desperately wants to fit in and later live a 'normal life', just like his peers.

We have experienced challenges around his disability, in particular accessing education, but also around racial profiling. Sometimes, especially when it comes to challenging things that haven't gone correctly, we find ourselves deciphering whether bias or discrimination are due to his race, or because of his disability. This can be challenging to unpick.

What have the last 2 years been like for you, since early 2020 when the COVID-19 Pandemic started?
I have found it extremely challenging, as my son's GCSE's have taken place during the pandemic, and GCSE's are difficult for literal thinkers. The wording in the exam questions and seeing the end point, which is quite important, is not straightforward when you're autistic.

This was further complicated by COVID constantly changing what was going to be expected. I needed to fully understand what was going to be expected of my son as he needs a month's worth of coaching and support to understand and prepare himself for change. This wasn't possible. That was undoubtedly hard for him too. He's fought for his education and worked as hard as he could, then came out with nothing because the goalposts had been moved. It felt really unfair.

We've had lots of discussions about what the actual point of going to school was. As things are, I'm struggling to see any point in it for some young people, other than to give them quite a harsh life lesson of how unfair the world's going to be outside of your home.

I'm not going to comment on the Bristol contacts, because there's lots of things that need to be fixed, but they're not just local to Bristol. And that's particularly relevant in terms of accessing education, whether you have additional needs or are a child of colour.

We have experienced incidents where racial stereotypes have been applied, which has led to a delay in accessing and obtaining help for his actual disability. One of them was an interesting situation where the school took legal action, where they racially profiled my son, they called social care, convinced that my son lived in a stereotypically dysfunctional black family.

This caused a delay to accessing an assessment for about 18 months while they kept calling social services. Social services were brilliant, they helped out and gave them (the school) a kick up the backside. But those things shouldn't happen. I'm well educated. I'm good at challenging systems. But if you are not in that position, particularly if English is not your first language, people just play with you, to be quite honest. They know the game, they know what they're doing. I could never believe that. It was an unwritten rule and it was deliberate.

But I guess with all of this, it's very, very isolating as a parent. Other parents that have never been through any form of discrimination will be like, "Oh, surely you haven't done this", or "have you not tried that", or whatnot. In the end, I just disengaged. The only people that I tend to have contact with are other people that have faced discrimination, and that's because they don't look at me as someone that hasn't tried hard enough.

As a parent, I've been aware of my son's autism since he was 4 years old. And I can tell you the amount of learning that I still do on a daily basis around autism is a lot. When parents imply you're not trying, or to go and speak to your MP, it's like, do you know how many times I've written to an MP? There's an assumption that you're stupid, or you're not doing something that you should have done. That makes me feel quite isolated.

But as I said, that's not a Bristol thing. That's just society, and people's attitudes as a whole. I guess for myself and my family, we would just like to live in peace. We'd like to have a normal, peaceful life, where we can go to work, or college or school or whatever it is, and just be accepted. To be allowed to access the normal things like education and employment, that anyone else can access without barriers.

What are you most excited or concerned about?

I have no clue what I'm most excited about. In this context, I guess what I'm most concerned about is that things don't change. That there will be a percentage of society that are just left behind because they fall into a group that can be discriminated against.

I'm going to lump together discrimination, just for the sake of it, it is just the principle of discriminating. Until we get rid of that mindset, as a society, there will always be a group of people that this is targeted at. I don't know why, but a lot of human beings seem naturally inclined to create biases and use those biases to inform their decisions, which ultimately ends up discriminating against people. Usually the people that you know least about get targeted, but this just shows a lack of understanding. So I guess my concern going forward is that things don't change.

What would you do if you had a magic wand?

If I had a magic wand, I would definitely cast a spell that stopped someone's mind - I'd design a pill that fixed the part of your brain that does the sorting for you. It's often not very useful sorting, and it would mean we could just accept people for who they are, as long as they're not causing any harm.

I always say to people, that as long as people aren't causing any harm, then actually what they're doing is none of your business. So you're the problem if you're concerning yourself with their business in any way.

What's the hardest thing you've learned?

The hardest thing I've learned is that the world and society are unfair, that there are people that are going to live life without jobs and without education through absolutely no fault of their own.

The other thing is, we all have a right to be angry, I feel that about the way that many of us have been treated. But then, especially as a black person, if I express any anger or frustration, ultimately, I'm seen as the angry black woman, and my son, oh, he's an angry black male. So we are seen as aggressive. The fact is that we're raising something that's happened to us. That's really not on.

I went through the care system, I was abused, sometimes I have issues as a result of that. I can be triggered by certain things that may lead to an expression of dissatisfaction with something in a rather direct way.

It's not aggressive, I would say that I just use plain direct language, it's not like I'm swearing, or being threatening or anything. But it's always perceived as that, which then makes me feel that we haven't got a right to have a voice, or to have emotions.

No one apologises for any of the bad things that have happened, or anything like that. All they quite often say is, "Well, did you not try this?" Or, "have you not tried that?" And it's tough to be forced into defending a position rather than being heard.

I'm going to be totally honest, I enjoyed being a parent and I love my child, I love him to bits, but I failed. I failed as a parent because I couldn't keep him safe, couldn't protect him and couldn't give him the life he's entitled to, especially when it came to education. I felt there was nothing I could physically do to make it better.

I've been one of those people that sent their child to school, feeling awful, feeling that I'm sending my child to school to be abused.

Not being able to fully protect my child once they entered the education or work world was probably the most surprising thing I discovered about being a parent. You think there are systems and processes in place to protect you? That's not really the case. They're just there as a fallback. For example, they say: "Well, we do have this policy or that policy in place, but whether you enforce them or not is another question altogether."

What's the hardest thing?

Being a parent is definitely the hardest thing I think I've ever had to do.

Who or what helps you most?

Who and what helps me the most is a very close circle of friends and family. And the fact that my son is so amazingly resilient, through all of all of this; that's probably what helps me most.

I'm inspired by people that I come into contact with that just keep going, despite all the challenges they quite clearly have. It's amazing when they do this positively as well, which is something that I sometimes struggle with, because it's not a positive experience. So I refuse to pretend that it's positive. Some of my close colleagues are just totally amazing when it comes to that, and their positivity quite often can act as a pick-me-up.

My biggest influence is definitely my son. What I would say to parents in similar situations is to forget about embarrassment, we need to move away from feeling that we can't talk about things.

I work with lots of young people, some of who got involved in criminal activities. They're all absolutely lovely people. They found themselves in situations quite often surrounded by fear. We've all acted out of fear in a way that may be classed as embarrassing. But I would say, be honest, and never, ever be embarrassed by anything that your child has done, whether it be good or bad, because it's part of learning, and part of life.

There are places that you can go for support and connection, I would say the best places quite often are social media groups with other parents and families. There are some amazing people that have knowledge of how they've tackled things that can really provide gems. No one there judges you. That's the amazing thing.

Everyone's been through stuff and no one is there to judge you, or suggest that you haven't tried anything.

Are there any gaps?

I would say the gaps are in our own individual attitudes, we need to question why we are judging and discriminating when we actually don't really understand the situation.

What we should be doing is sitting there thinking that we're very lucky and very privileged to have never gone through that, and offering empathy rather than judgment and discrimination.

I'll be totally honest, and this sounds really, really harsh and sad, and I will reiterate, it has nothing to do with my son who I love to bits, but I would actually consider very carefully if I would want to be a parent again. I have one child. I may never have a second child because I don't believe I can protect them. It's very, very hard. But you sit here and you think I actually put my child here in this world to face that. I am part of the problem. And now I know that I cannot protect a child from these external factors, I would really consider whether it is a fair thing to put a child in that situation. It's not something that I would do given the choice again, because it's quite a tough thing to live with and the buck stops with you.

Where can people connect with you?

If people want to connect with me, LinkedIn is probably the best place.

Things to look out for?

I will provide some information about the awards and a couple of groups that have been absolutely amazing. They have provided me support while I've been going through and sharing information and knowledge.

My work and experience

Some of my experience is working with other young people. There's a lot about knife crime at the moment, right? There's this huge belief that these children are evil or dangerous children, they're not. They are lovely young people, they are terrified.

I took a knife off of my son. And it's a very, very common thing. And there's a lot of parents that will sit there and go, "Oh my God!"

Children are terrified of walking around the streets at the moment, absolutely terrified. So out of fear, they are arming themselves. That's quite a normal reaction for a young person, or actually, for a lot of older people as well, that if in fear, you attempt to defend yourself. A lot of people are just not talking about this, and at the moment it is very hard to find support for parents. It's very hard to say, "You know what I found, I found a knife on my child this morning". Because everyone's like, "Oh, my God, your child's in a gang." But they're just scared to walk to the shop.

It is a failing on the part of society that children do not feel safe to walk around.

And I bet you any amount of money, that if you stopped and searched a lot of women, given the rates of sexual offenses at the moment, that they'd have some form of weapon. It may not be a knife but it may be a can of deodorant - I used to carry one in my bag when I was younger to spray in a man's face if they attacked you. The bottom line is people feel a lack of safety on our streets. It is leading to a real ramp up of a very dangerously negative stereotype that seems to be hitting ethnic minority children and children that live in poorer white areas.

The police think the streets aren't safe. And people may say, "Oh, it's not the police's responsibility. It's the parents". But actually, my son said something to me which hit home. He said, "Mum, would you rather visit me at the cemetery or in a police cell?" I can always trust my son to challenge me and if it comes down to it, I'd rather visit him in a police cell than in a cemetery.

There was a lyric in a song, one of the young people songs that I listened to, that said, "I'd rather be judged by twelve than carried by six," and it's quite right. If you actually believe you're going to lose your life, then prison seems like an easier option. This is all around fear.

But the issue is it's a buried conversation that is not really happening. Because it depends on parents opening up and sharing experiences that they've had quite often with their young person. They either don't want people to know or they're very scared of it getting out there and affecting their children for the rest of their lives.

It's a really, really hard one and then you've the added layer of ethnic minorities, or disabilities or both. And then it all gets muddled with, "Oh, but they're in a gang". But yeah, they're in a gang because no one else accepted them. So they've joined a group of other misfits for their own safety. So what? What do we want them to do?

The only thing I would say is that none of this makes you a bad parent. The only thing that makes you a bad parent is if you're judging other parents.

"Every parent is different and so is every child, so you can read all the books and scribble down all the advice you want, but you're not going to know what to do until you've got that baby in your arms. And even then you still might not know — and that's totally OK!"

Kelly Rowland

HELEN NEALE

Helen Neale runs the KiddyCharts media site, which has been providing advice and activities to both parents and educators for over 10 years. This is the only social business in the parenting media space, giving 51%+ profit to charity every year. KiddyCharts offers resources to both educate and entertain kids, often with a focus on their wellbeing as well as their learning.

Helen is passionate about helping kids to grow and reach their full potential by empowering them to help themselves through both understanding and expressing their emotions. She is a qualified Level 3 CPCAB counsellor, and a member of the BACP. She volunteers as a counsellor for a children's charity in the UK. She also has two teenage kids of her own.

Connect with Helen:
Website: www.kiddycharts.com
Twitter: www.twitter.com/kiddycharts
Facebook: www.facebook.com/kiddycharts
Instagram: www.instagram.com/kiddycharts
Pinterest: www.pinterest.com/kiddycharts

Five Reasons Why it's OK to Admit Parenting is Tough Sometimes

Let's start by saying that being a parent is wonderful. However, sometimes it is OK to not like it. In fact, it is normal to feel like this. We can't all be shouting from the rooftops about how awesome the whole parenting gig is, and not admitting to struggling sometimes. There are many that would LOVE to be lucky and have healthy and happy children. But does that mean that it isn't **allowed** for parents to admit that it can be pretty damn tough? Can we admit that we want to fecking run away from it all completely sometimes and read a book without having to think about the next thing that needs doing as a parent, or the threat of another *"mummy"* whine from the three year old?

We've taken a step back from the daily struggle of being a mum to try and think about **why** it is OK to admit that being a parent isn't great sometimes. It IS tough but we are all in it together.

It takes a village to raise a child. Let's work together to raise our kids, offering support and kindness every step of the way.

It Doesn't Mean You Don't Love Them

When parenting, sometimes tough choices have to be made, including making decisions that aren't popular with the children. This can cause them to be angry, defiant, and sometimes extremely hurtful in that moment:

"You don't love me otherwise you wouldn't do that!"

"I hate you!"

Say teens, and kids the world over….

It can be really hurtful when they say these things. Parents can feel upset and cross. Feeling this doesn't mean our children aren't liked or loved, it just means that the way they **are behaving** isn't acceptable.

That is 100 percent fine, and 100 percent normal too.

It is hard not to take things personally, but know this emotion from your children will pass. Particularly if, as parents, thought is given as to **why** these emotions have boiled over in our children. Do they feel listened to? Is there something else going on? It is also worth noting that if children speak to us like this, it can often mean that they feel secure in the knowledge that you WILL love them, no matter what – unconditionally.

It Doesn't Mean That You Think They Are a Burden

Sometimes it can be hard to parent in a crisis, particularly if your child feels like they need constant attention. Perhaps you want a break from having to help a child with special needs, or just want to not hear the phrase "mummy" again for five minutes.

Just wanting a little bit of me time is important for functioning properly. Me time is part of self-care for mums.

"Until you have a kid with special needs you have no idea of the depth of your strength, tenacity and resourcefulness." - Anonymous

Giving yourself time for self-care means better parenting overall, whatever the challenges faced.

You Are Only Human

Nobody is able to function on reduced sleep, especially in a tense environment when conflict happens, without experiencing a gamut of emotions.

You are human. Humans were made to **feel**, so the positive moments of parenting cannot come without those negative moments too. For a child to show joy and love, they also need to have space and safety to show fear, anger and hurt.

The same is true for us. Embrace humanity. It makes us, and our children, the wonderful people we are, and what we hope for all of us to be.

"Without pain, how could we know joy?" - John Green, The Fault in Our Stars

This is simplistic; to experience the good, the bad must be felt too.

Anyone who has spent time hugging children after a tantrum will have had the realisation that all they really needed was love. It is important to remember that if children are acting up, they may be looking for a way to connect, and that post-tantrum hug can provide this opportunity for them.

Acknowledging Feelings Helps You to Work With Them

If you KNOW you are feeling upset and finding things tough, then you can work with it. **Saying** how you feel can actually help so much in dealing with those emotions giving you strategies to cope.

Have you ever thought back on your day and all the emotions you felt? Have you named those emotions? You might be surprised how hard you have to think to name a few, even from the last 24 hours.

Give it a go, and think about the positive emotions too.

Understanding how you feel can help give you power over those emotions, enabling more control.

Psychologist Dan Siegel even refers to this practice as:

"Name it to tame it." - Dan Seigel

So yes, parenting is tough, and it might make you angry, sad, happy, disappointed, thoughtful, confused, pleased, proud, and overwhelmed. Sometimes all in the space of five minutes, but if you acknowledge this, you're actually *winning*!

Nobody is Perfect

Lastly, nobody gets it right ALL the time. We learn by making mistakes. So make them, learn from them, move on, and perhaps we can all accept that **parenting is imperfect perfection**!

"It is time for parents to teach young people that in diversity there is beauty and there is strength."

Maya Angelou

The ONE Thing That Helps You Understand Your Kids More Than Anything

We've already talked about how tough it is being a parent. And that it is OK to admit to yourself and others that you are finding it a cold, hard slog raising these complicated little people.

But what if there was something, within your power, that could make a big difference in helping you to really understand your child?

It's a six letter word.

LISTEN.

I realise that this might be stating the obvious, but tell me when was the last time that you really did LISTEN to your child, and I mean was really, truly, completely present just for them?

Learning to be Truly Present When Your Child Talks to You

Life is pretty busy as a parent, isn't it? There are surfaces to clean, pants to wash, LEGO® to pick up off the floor, work that needs to be planned, and payments for trips that need to be made.

The list is endless. Once you tick one thing off, there is something else that takes its place. The to-do list of any parent or carer is a living, breathing being that sometimes you fear will completely engulf you. There are a million and one things that are whizzing around your head on a daily basis that are part of that to-do list.

Thoughts are wonderful things. The right thought at the right time can make a person's day, and bring a smile to a loved one's face.

But, overthinking can be disruptive and distracting.

Too much negative talk about ourselves, too often, can sabotage our mental health, and turn the brightest spark into a much dimmer light.

If we aren't really present when our kids are talking to us, we are neither helping ourselves nor them.

It is our thoughts and deeds that control if we are present, so before you take time to listen to your children:

- Put down your phone.
- Turn off the television or PC.
- Stop ruminating about what happened with your friends yesterday.
- Shelve thinking about that report you need to finish for work.

That way you can truly listen to your child when they are speaking to you.

We know this isn't feasible **all** the time. But the more you take time to be present, and mindful in those conversations with your children, the easier it becomes to understand them.

Through those conversations you can get to know what really matters to them. That might be about how important it is to them to be able to put on their own shoes, or that they want the unicorn cake for pudding, or that they're really scared of a test they are going to have tomorrow.

Big or small, be present for them, and you'll be able to understand just what your child is saying about how they **feel**.

When you are there for the little things, they are so much more likely to trust that you will be there for the bigger things as they grow older.

And for a child, the little things **are** big things, aren't they?

If you are present and completely engaged, that will make the next step all the more easier to manage.

Try Not to Make it About You

When you were last out with your friends explaining how something that has happened to you was uber-frustrating, was there a lot of this going on?

"Oh don't worry. I remember that happening to me, it was…."

"Totally get that, we found that when that started for us, it felt…."

"Oh you think that was bad, when it happened to us, we found it was five-times worse because…."

Friends listen, and they relate to what's happening to you all the time, and sometimes it's just what you need, but…

Sometimes you just want your friends to **listen**.

To nod and show clear and present interest in what you are saying.

To commiserate with you, tell you that it sounds like it's been a bit crap, and maybe even give you a hug; as long as you are comfortable with that.

We want to feel **connected** with those friends.

What is it about all these responses that doesn't really help or support you?

In trying to **identify** with your situation, they make it all about **them**, and not about you, and how **you** are feeling about what has happened.

Imagine you are a nine-year-old child, and you are really struggling in school.

Really Imagine

You can't pluck up the courage to talk to people in your new class, and it is making you feel really lonely and sad whenever you go into school.

You have been worrying about it for weeks, and you pluck up the courage to tell your carer, or one of your parents.

And they say:

"Oh don't worry, it'll be fine in a couple of weeks. It's always difficult when you are new. I remember when I started a new school,

and I sat and ate lunch all on my own for weeks. I got over it though. It'll all be forgotten in a bit and be back to normal again."

Reassurance, at the surface of it, is giving them confidence that there is nothing to worry about, and this is completely understandable to do as a parent. We draw on our own experiences, and offer sympathy to our children for how they are feeling.

But, does this response take into account what that little, vulnerable nine-year-old is feeling right now? Does it help them to work out what **they** want to happen?

Does it help them express how they're feeling?

And finally, does it empower them to work towards a plan so they can find a solution to their worries?

Avoid Blocking That Crucial Empathy for Your Child

Once you stop identifying with your child's needs and start really listening to what they're telling you, you can explore how **they** are feeling. Not how you felt when it happened to **you**.

It is 100 percent probable that whatever you felt isn't exactly the same as how your child is feeling.

Our kids are **not** us in smaller bodies. They think, feel, and react differently according to their own wants, personalities, needs, and ideas.

If you manage to take that step back, to stop identifying and begin offering sympathy, you will be completely connected to them and be able to express **empathy** for their situation.

You aren't thinking about how you felt when that happened to you. You are simply trying to understand how they feel now it is happening to them.

If we can't push past our own experiences to fully take in the experiences of our own children, we cannot hope to understand and empathise with how they are feeling about those experiences.

If we don't have that empathy, we aren't empowering our kids to understand those feelings, and learn to deal with them.

The power that being heard empathetically creates in our children is phenomenal.

A much better response to that nine year old might be:

"It seems as though you are having a difficult time at school at the moment, and it's making you feel sad and lonely when you go in."

We have acknowledged how they feel. We have told them that we have heard, and we have accepted them and the feelings that they have had.

Just a single sentence that allows the child to understand how they feel, to hold them in that moment, creates a feeling of safety and being seen. Helping them to understand how they're feeling, so you can further understand and support them as well.

Next time you chat to your children:
Listen. Actively.
Try not to identify.
Hold the space they are talking in, so they feel safe.

You'll be amazed at how that acceptance will empower and help them make sense of their own world, and bring you both closer together.

For further reading, this book is amazing for helping kids, and even adults, to understand the difference between sympathy and empathy, which really allows us to truly listen and be present for our children when they are ready: https://amzn.to/3KRoCWr (this is an affiliate link).

"Parenthood...It's about guiding the next generation, and forgiving the last."

Pete Krause

JANE EVANS

International Parenting Coach and Media Expert, Jane Evans, famously known for going head-to-head live on Good Morning Britain TV with an irate Piers Morgan! Jane credits her son, the children, young people, parents, and carers she's worked with and cared for, as being her greatest teachers. They have consistently shown and taught her the realities of how lives are profoundly shaped by early childhood experiences.

Jane's huge curiosity about the *why* behind children and adults struggles with anxiety and low self-worth has led her to study a wide range of cutting-edge body and brain-based science. And to create four children's books so that parents, carers, and professionals have essential resources to use with the children.

Jane brings her knowledge, her professional and life experience into her roles as a renowned TV and Radio Expert, author of four children's' books, her TED Talk, and her international Coaching and speaking. Jane is a co-creator of the highly effective Healing Together Programme in partnership with the ground-breaking Innovating Minds.

Jane regularly trains those working directly with children to offer a trauma-sensitive programme with resources to support children impacted by domestic violence, anxiety, and overwhelming feelings of anger.

Jane makes the *why* behind children and adult's behaviours, simple to grasp, and provides solid, practical solutions so everyone has the opportunity to live well, beyond their anxiety and other limiting beliefs and behaviours.

Connect with Jane:

Website: www.thejaneevans.com

Email: jane@thejaneevans.com

Twitter: @janeparenting2

Facebook: www.facebook.com/parentingbeyondanxiety

Jane's TED Talk is Taming and Tending Your Meerkat Brain

Jane's books published by Jessica Kingsley Publishers:

Little Meerkat's Big Panic

How Are You Feeling Today Baby Bear?

Cyril Squirrel Finds Out About Love

Kit Kitten and the Topsy-Turvy Feelings

Parenting

You may be fairly new to parenting, or you may have been doing it for a long time now. It's an ongoing journey, so what you are doing will always be important. You may have come to parenting biologically, within a relationship, or by leaning into the many ways it's now possible to create and nurture life. Or in a way that's too hard or painful to think about, or you chose to become a parent via adoption, or by being a family member who has become a kinship carer. You may be parenting as part of your role as a grandparent, foster carer, stepparent, aunt, uncle, or close friend.

Parenting matters, parents matter, and most of all children matter! Children are the next generation who will be present in our world and shape it profoundly. Raising children is the most important thing anyone will do, despite the lack of status that parenting continues to have in our world.

I'm wondering if, at any point on your parenting journey, you were told that parenting is really about 'relationshipping?' Research conducted by Bowlby, Ainsworth and others on mother and child attachment in the 1940's was showing us this very clearly but sadly it got a bit lost along the way. Taken over by an emphasis on 'good children' and managing behaviour, it shifted focus towards teaching right from wrong, how to respect others, learn, have good manners, listen, and do tasks when asked to. All of these have served to hijack the relationship with your child, and sadly has made getting children to comply into the jewel in the crown for them and for you.

My son taught me to put our relationship first about 30 years ago. When I focused on his behaviour and tried to manipulate him with rewards, consequences, or praise, it was like putting him on the other side of a deep, murky river. It felt horrible for us both. Miserable, pointless and a lonely disconnection. But if I focused on keeping us connected whilst showing I most cared about his feelings more than his behaviour, it felt great and gave the best opportunities to learn together. And, when he could, he joined in with being curious about his feelings as the foundation for his emotional growth. It wasn't plain sailing of course, as he's a living being and at that stage had very limited impulse control (the part of the brain that develops way into adulthood!).

Fortunately, parenting or relationshipping is ALWAYS a work in progress. So allow yourself a sigh of relief as it's never too early, or too late to shift your focus from managing and controlling behaviour to putting your child, their feelings, and your relationship with them first.

The wonderful benefits of having a focus on the relationships we offer and create with our children, is that it really nurtures their mental and physical health. It broadens their access to learning, friendships, and relationships far better than anything else. It also gives them the ability to slowly learn what it feels like when they are not feeling emotionally and physically calm and safe, and to restore this so they can get on with enjoying their life. Which is the foundation for all we dream of for our children.

Now, if you are thinking you're not sure that you did focus on 'relationshipping' thus far on your parenting journey - do NOT panic! The joy of parenting is that it's an ongoing experience so it's never too late to change how you interact with your child. It turns out (thanks to the current research on brain and body science we now have) that all the other parenting stuff can come after we prioritise the relationships we create with our children. This approach to parenting is a way of teaching and correcting manners, learning how to cross the road, take a turn, tidy a room, tell the truth and much more. Through relational, relationship first parenting we can model and safely guide children. In fact we do this anyway, often without realising it.

From conception babies are on a HUGE 'how to be a human' learning curve because human babies are born way before their brains are developed. Fortunately in order to learn how to stand, walk, talk, hold things, and zillions of other stuff, babies and young children initially have brains that are super absorbent sponges. They have nearly 87 billion brain cells to connect together – which, on reflection, is a slightly scary thought, because in the first few years of life, what happens to, and around them all goes quickly and deeply in as unfiltered truth about themselves, relationships with others and their world.

Current science that shows the power and benefits of nurturing the connection and relationship with a child as the foundation for all they need began to seep into my parenting, fostering, and coaching. Slowly but surely as it felt so right and made total sense! It has profoundly changed everything forever. It's what I continue to use with my son and my new granddaughter, and in all the coaching and training I do with parents, carers, and professionals. It's a different way of parenting that's informed by and aligns with how brains and bodies actually develop and work. And what's extra fascinating is that 'relationshipping' is much more in line with how our ancient ancestors raised children. How ironic we needed the last 30 years of new science and technology to look inside of developing brains and bodies to affirm what nature intended. To come full circle and arrive at this amazing place of putting the relationship at the heart of parenting.

What does this look like in day to day parenting? It involves putting the connection and relationship with your child, of any age, first. Is all about repeatedly bringing a baby or child back to feeling calm and safe again. Anyone who has ever tried to do that to a 3 year old who has just dropped their ice cream, or with a teenager who has been asked to turn off their phone to go to sleep, will know this is not easy to do! But, by calming yourself so you can genuinely care about how this might **feel** for them is what will support the child to have the smoothest experience. Through this, they will feel safe enough to show and share their feelings about what's happening in that moment with you (which will really help them as adults). You are putting the feelings they are, understandably, having first, rather than your need to stop them crying or yelling 'no!'

In reality, in these moments of high emotion in the child that we are attempting to parent, all too often, the wheels tend to come off **our** trolley! Even with the best of intentions we get flicked into a state of fight or flight, shutdown or withdrawal. Which means we tend to talk at them, rather than calm ourselves FIRST – the old put your oxygen mask on first analogy – literally you need to BREATHE several times. We do this to avoid dumping them on the other, lonely side of the deep, murky river, into full on lecturing, rationalising and fixing mode.

The super short version of this is –

BREATHE, BREATHE, BREATHE! Until you can speak kindly and be kind!

Once calm, you can be authentically curious about how they are feeling first.

This enables them to feel that they, and their feelings, matter. The repeated experience of this will be an amazing foundation for their mental and emotional health for life.

This puts the relationship with them centre stage, always!

You might need to explore feelings you have from them yelling at you, avoid shaming them or it'll do more harm than any good.

And of course, a light mention of, "Because I know you know that yelling isn't OK. So how can I help?" (They do know so we don't need to labour the point, they are struggling to 'do' what they know.)

The reality is that children are very young when they start learning what adults find acceptable and what ruffles their feathers, but their underdeveloped brains have no impulse control to stop themselves from pushing, biting, or yelling. That's where putting your relationship with them first and having a calm, kind connection comes in so beautifully.

Parenting and 'relationshipping' is a whole community commitment that everyone needs to embrace. Ideally it happens within a tribe. So let's be that tribe, because raising children can often feel like a tough, lonely path that you are on for a looooooong time! We all have opportunities to support anyone who is parenting, whether it's by sharing a kind smile or word with the parent or grandparent you meet on a walk, or letting them go in front of you in a queue, or standing back so they can get by with their buggy. If we take a moment to acknowledge, connect with and truly see the parent as well as the child, it gives them a sense of how much they matter and are valued. It gives them a droplet of, "I see you and you matter", which is what 'relationshipping' is all about.

"By loving them for more than their abilities, we show our children that they are much more than the sum of their accomplishments."

Eileen Kennedy-Moore

LIZ WALTON

Liz Walton is a therapist, coach, trainer and facilitator. With 27 years in the industry of health wellness and therapy, she has a lot of modalities to pull from. These include massage, hypnotherapy journey work, past life regression, NLP timeline therapy, EFT known as tapping, matrix bursary and printing and going into patterns, genealogy and family constellation work. I work with the mind body connection to facilitate a healthy path in life. We have the answers inside and how we can best connect to our true selves.

Liz helps women who are struggling to get or stay pregnant, or if they have reached the point where it is time to let go. How does she do this? What makes her different from others in this field is her personal story of 10 years: 6 IVF cycles, $60k and doing everything in her power to find the key. She knew she had to let it all go and give up, after her sister in law fell pregnant the first time with IVF. Then 3 years later, she fell pregnant naturally and had a baby at the age of 46. Her experience means she can give clients the best possible chances of reaching their desired outcomes of a family or a life that they always wanted.

Liz has travelled all of her life and lived in many countries. This has given her a passion for people and a love of life.

Although she has a focus on fertility, this is not the only coaching she does. She specialises in grief, depression and abuse. Liz works with the deep emotional aspects of our beings, to enable clients to unpack their emotional baggage so they don't have to carry it around anymore.

'The Journey' is a globally recognized, critically acclaimed, healing and transformation methodology. It works fast to awaken you to your limitless potential – so you can achieve success in every area of your life.

You can use 'The Journey' for both physical and emotional healing. It's proven successful with all kinds of physical ailments, emotional issues, depression, relationship issues, career blocks and many of life's other challenges.

With Matrix Birth Reimprinting you can go back to the womb and reimprint your birth experience, which will change your energy levels, mood, and wellbeing in the present. Matrix Birth Reimprinting is a specially designed technique developed by Sharon King. Using elements of EFT and Matrix Reimprinting, we can go back and release the emotions connected to these traumas and create a whole new experience and belief system. With these gentle, yet powerful protocols, we can recreate the birth process and experience the special bonding process that is natural to every mother and child.

Connect with Liz:
Website: www.magicalnewbeginnings.com
Facebook: www.facebook.com/LizWaltonfertilitycoach/
Instagram: @Lizwalton_fertilitycoach

Fertility, Health and Coming Back to the Self

I have been on quite a journey of health and healing myself. From being a very scared, shy, lost soul to now feeling confident in my power and using it to support other women to come home to their true selves. Coming home to who I truly am has probably been the most liberating experience that I could have ever done for myself. And now with 27 years behind me of training, learning, growing and experiencing, plus my own personal journey, I now get to help and support other people on their journeys, as well as always continuing my journey of love and peace.

My most recent journey has been of fertility. I had a 10 year fertility journey which included six IVF treatments, trying to do everything in my power to find out what was wrong with me. Then realizing that I really needed to let go of my dream of ever becoming a parent, because I needed my sanity more. The next part of my journey was to become whole, let go and accept life and the joy that it really brings. This culminated in having a child 3 years later, at the age of 46. Now 52 with a 6 year old, I can bless my 10 year journey and bless all of my learnings before, because everything up until now has enabled me to embody who I truly am so I can help others to do the same.

I am now a Fertility Coach working in the area of creation and supporting women, men and couples of all shapes, sizes and flavours when it comes to the area of fertility. To me, fertility doesn't always mean just having a baby. I not only support women that struggle to get pregnant, but also around staying pregnant, or when it's time to let go and stop trying. Fertility also includes grief, stress, anxiety and depression – to name a few symptoms that can come from being on a fertility journey.

I work in the mind to body connection, the huge emotional journey, the roller coaster of life and of health fertility, aiming to bring the lives of those

I help back to themselves. It is important to realise that we are the treasure, creation is who we are, who we become and then from this we create.

I support my clients with the mental and emotional aspects of life. I deal with the layers underneath the symptoms, so that we can release the blocks in the way that stop us from creating. If our body is a mirror to what's going on in our mind, then by looking at the mind, and healing it, we can bring freedom and flow to the body.

One of my favourite sayings is 'when the student is ready. the teacher will appear', and this is what I felt happened to me when my daughter eventually came along. Once I had learned everything I had to learn and understood and really embodied who I was, it was like she looked down on me and said 'I can come in now she gets it'.

I stand here now as a woman, a coach, a mother and wife, able to share my experience both professionally and personally so I can support other people on their journey of creation, whether it be in health, fertility or self-actualisation. I think I have found my calling, all of my life, my ups and downs, my tough times all flow together to create the business that is my passion and my love, besides my daughter and my husband. Through everything I feel empowered to step outside into the world so I can be of service to others.

So if you're looking for a coach to support you, who has walked that path and understands all those emotions, then I'm here to serve.

In love and service, Liz Walton.

"Be the change you wish to see" - Ghandi

"As your kids grow up, they may forget what you said, but they won't forget how you made them feel."

Kevin Heath

AFTERWORD
By Sharon Critchlow

When we form our relationships and our families, we dream about how much love we have to give and how much love we will receive. People have a tendency to hold opinions about aspects of family life, influenced by whether they enjoyed a family life or not. This level of interest can give rise to pressure to parent in a certain way and sometimes can lead to guilt for not being a certain way, or to a feeling of failure. This is made harder when troubles arise and a pathway ahead looks less certain. These stories have taught us that there can be bumps in the road which can sometimes take half of a lifetime to overcome, but that there is always a way forward.

We hope that you see the brave humanity in these pages, as these authors share their hopes, fears and experiences. In these chapters we explore stories of becoming a parent in all of its forms, of ensuring help for our children through difficult times and of losing our children. Ultimately, we hear of how support through unimaginably difficulty can be found amongst the warm embrace of those around us. We have learned that parenting and being a family is not just within the realms of biology but that this love grows when the intention to step in to that place is taken. Our authors have shown time and time again that parenting is the ultimate act of love, it is the hardest job in the world and can also be one of the most rewarding.

I am reminded of a quote:

"It's not only children who grow. Parents do too. As much as we watch and see what our children do with their lives, they are watching us to see what we do with ours. I can't tell my children to reach for the sun. All I can do is reach for it myself." — Joyce Maynard

"A parent's love is whole no matter how many times divided."

Robert Brault

REFERENCES FOR UK AND US ORGANISATIONS

Autism
https://www.autism.org.uk/
https://www.facebook.com/groups/autismindependence

Post Natal Depression
https://apni.org/
https://www.postpartum.net/

Anxiety
https://www.anxietyuk.org.uk
https://adaa.org/

Child and Youth Mental Health
https://www.otrbristol.org.uk
https://www.childline.org.uk/
http://teenmentalhealth.org/

Suicide Prevention
https://www.spbristol.org
http://www.samaritans.org.uk or Call 116 123
https://www.papyrus-uk.org (People under 35)
https://www.samaritansusa.org/
https://suicidepreventionlifeline.org/

IBS
https://www.theibsnetwork.org/
https://www.ibspatient.org/

Endometriosis
https://www.endometriosis-uk.org/
http://www.endofound.org

Depression
http://www.mind.org.uk
https://www.dbsalliance.org/

Breast Cancer
https://breastcancernow.org/
https://www.nationalbreastcancer.org/

Cervical Cancer
https://www.jostrust.org.uk/get-support
https://www.nccc-online.org/

Menopause
https://menopausesupport.co.uk/
https://www.menopause.org/

Inflammatory Bowel Disease
https://www.crohnsandcolitis.org.uk
https://www.crohnscolitisfoundation.org

Stoma Awareness
https://www.colostomyuk.org/ (See also #StomaAware)
https://www.ostomy.org/

IVF
https://fertilitynetworkuk.org/
https://resolve.org/

Child Loss
https://www.cruse.org.uk
https://firstcandle.org/

Special Educational Needs and Disabilities (SEND)
https://www.bristolsendjustice.com
https://www.sendadvocacy.com

Sexual Abuse
https://www.thesurvivorstrust.org/
https://www.rainn.org/

Domestic Abuse
https://www.nationaldahelpline.org.uk
https://www.thehotline.org/

Support for 18 to 25 year olds from minority groups
https://www.facebook.com/groups/changeyourmindsetevolve

"What's it's like to be a parent. It's one of the hardest things you'll ever do but in exchange it teaches you the meaning of unconditional love."

Nicholas Sparks

ABOUT DISCOVER YOUR BOUNCE!

Discover Your Bounce is a group of companies to provide a platform for wellbeing and inspiration, to support each other and to learn from our collective experience.

Discover Your Bounce Publishing specialises in inspirational stories and business books. We provide writing courses, mentoring for authors and support from inception of your idea through writing, publishing and managing your book launch. If you have an idea for a book, or a part written manuscript that you want to get over the line, contact Nicky or Sharon on the links below.

Discover Your Bounce For Business provides support for employers who want to improve the staff wellbeing, engagement, culture and performance of their business. We work with CEOs, HR Managers or department heads to deliver workshops with practical, easy to implement techniques that create instant change. As we go to print, we have worked with over 4000 employees across the globe from a variety of industries and have delivered keynotes at some fantastic international conferences and events.

My Wellbeing supports individuals through mentoring and online courses to improve their energy and vision. If your get up and go has got up and gone, get in touch and get bouncing or choose your programme at www.discoveryourbounceacademy.com.

Sharon and Nicky are available to discuss speaking opportunities, wellbeing workshops or private mentoring:
Nicky@discoveryourbounce.com
Sharon@discoveryourbounce.com

You can also find out more on our website:
https://www.discoveryourbounce.com

JOIN OUR COMMUNITIES!
For wellbeing inspiration and positivity:
www.facebook.com/groups/discoveryourbouncecommunity

For book lovers:
www.facebook.com/groups/bouncybooks

THE BOUNCE BACK JOURNEY SERIES

The original Bounce Back Journey was published in February 2020, with no idea of the challenges that were to come. The series includes The Bounce Back Journey of Women's Health, The Bounce Back Journey of Men's Health, The Bounce Back Journey of Careers and so this book makes a perfect addition.

SOCIAL PASSION PROJECT
Royalties from these books fund our Social Passion Project, providing mental health awareness training and supporting other important mental health projects. Read more at:
www.discoveryourbounce.com/social-passion-project.